MORRIS AUTOMATED INFORMATION NETWORK

0 1029 0684068 5

Parsippany-Troy Hills Library
Main Library
449 Halsey RD
Parsippany NJ 07054
973-887-5150

LEARN

to

SAIL TODAY!

FROM NOVICE TO SAILOR IN ONE WEEK

D1609268

NOV 2 2 2016

Sailing on Lake Michigan with Chicago skyline in the distance. (Photo courtesy of Charles Jiminez collection, Ryan Williams photographer)

LEARN
to
SAIL TODAY!
FROM NOVICE TO SAILOR IN ONE WEEK

Commodore Barry Lewis

New York | Chicago | San Francisco | Athens | London | Madrid |
Mexico City | Milan | New Delhi | Singapore | Sydney | Toronto

Copyright © 2016 by McGraw-Hill Education. All rights reserved.
Printed in the United States of America. Except as permitted under the
United States Copyright Act of 1976, no part of this publication may be
reproduced or distributed in any form or by any means, or stored in a data
base or retrieval system, without prior written permission of the publisher.

1 2 3 4 5 6 7 8 9 QFR 21 20 19 18 17 16

ISBN   978-0-07-183088-1
MHID   0-07-183088-X

e-Book ISBN   0-07-183089-8
e-Book MHID   978-0-07-183089-8

Photographs are by the author unless otherwise noted.

McGraw-Hill Education books are available at special quantity discounts
to use as premiums and sales promotions, or for use in corporate training
programs. To contact a representative, please visit the Contact Us page at
http://www.mhprofessional.com/

CONTENTS

ACKNOWLEDGMENTS

This book is dedicated to those who sailed to sea in more dangerous times seeking knowledge or fortune, knowing not what lay ahead. It is also dedicated to the people who taught me to sail. Members of the Evanston Sailing Club (of Illinois), I have forgotten your names, but not your deeds. Bob Benson, skipper of *Wolf*, the Chicago Yacht Club's rookie J/24 boat of the year in 1980 (co-winner with *Perdido*). I never again had a captain the likes of you. My crew on *Raven*: Paul Hydzik and Bob Kenny. Seldom has a captain learned so much from his crew; they are why *Raven* was such a terror on the racecourse. Thanks to Waukegan Yacht Club, its Swing Keel Regatta, and the South Coast Sailing Club for all that nice hardware. I keep it on display. It all really belongs to my crew.

Thanks to the Belmont Yacht Club and Northwest Sailing Association for their members' trust and support.

This book is not the work of one person. Countless articles and books have been scoured over the years and numerous seminars attended. I am fortunate to have the support of my two wonderful children, Rachel and Seth, my mother, Ruth, and many good friends, all of whose unfailing support of this endeavor made it possible. Several people took the time to read the entire book just because I asked. Leon Anderson was the first to review it. His encouragement and suggestions were fantastic, his enthusiasm, contagious. Jane McMillan searched through the book for things to be improved and offered more encouragement. John Williams, John Graneto, Denise

Olhava, Mark Stein, Donna Masterson, Jan Suberman, Paul Hydzik, Estee Jacob, Dr. Susan Benjamin Feingold: thank you all. This book has been blessed with the finest set of editors imaginable. Molly Mulhern was the first editor to whom this manuscript was submitted. I am grateful beyond words for both her praise and her criticism. Her vision of this book differed from mine and improved it beyond measure. Christopher Brown, Janet Robbins, and Cathy Kulka invested a great amount of time and with their sharp editors' eyes and minds made many improvements. Thanks also to some relatives of mine who showed the way by getting their own productions published: Danny Newman, my cousin; Hershel Lewis, my uncle; Melvin Lewis, my father; Ruth Lewis, my mother; and some others I'd include except for the fear I'd be accused of merely name dropping. Many thanks Dan Caplan, Paul Bowen, Katie Colgan, Charlie Jiminez, Ryan Williams, Dan Waters, the Jacobs/Caplans for their photos, and Clare Rosean and Christopher Hoyt for the art.

The author gratefully acknowledges the technical assistance of Douglas Nesbitt, a photographer in Orlando, Florida. Many thanks to Maryann Karinch for arriving in the nick of time with encouragement and helpful suggestions.

A brief word on pronouns: There is no sexist intent in the use herein of pronouns. The male pronoun is used only to avoid cumbersome language, not to insult the great female skippers I have met or whose fascinating exploits I only could read about.

And, finally, with thanks to Markus Zusak. I, too, have loved these words and hope I have made them right.

INTRODUCTION

> *"I love sailing. You will too. Join me today!"*

Y ou have picked up this book because sailing intrigues you. That is the first step to becoming a sailor. This is the only book that can take you from landlubber to novice sailor, safely, today. *Learn to Sail Today!* requires no memorization. Your common sense, and the essential skills from this book, will get you out on the water and safely back. Today!

You will learn to sail today much as you learned to ride a bicycle. Most people learned at a young age, taught by siblings or parents. You may have been told something like, "Put your feet on these pedals, and hold onto this thing with both hands. Now push down on the pedals and make the bike move. If you start to fall left, turn left. If you start to fall right, turn right." Soon it became easy, even for a preschooler.

Once you learned to balance, you were immediately taught to brake and turn. At this stage, you safely enjoyed riding your bike in a park, or on a driveway. Other skills were learned over time.

You did not need to memorize that what you were holding onto were the handlebars, or that there are three basic types of handlebars. You just needed to hold on and turn them. Balance soon became intuitive. Stepping on the pedals turned the wheels; that was intuitive as well. The brakes stopped the bike; your knowledge of friction was intuitive. Safety was addressed simply by limiting you to the safest nearby location, helping you into your helmet, and telling you to stop or turn away from anything and everything in your way. The entire teaching process was simplified and intuitive. That teaching method works well because our minds are set up to learn intuitively and one step at a time, not by memorization.

Let us learn to sail the same way you learned bicycling: one step at a time, with the thrill of success on your first day.

As a beginner's book, *Learn to Sail Today!* is intended to give you a solid foundation for your increasingly adventurous sails. Sailing terms are mentioned in this book, but feel free to ignore the terms for now. The terminology is not essential for the beginner, but you will be more comfortable knowing some basic terms when you sail along with others. The sailing terms do allow for unambiguous, simple orders. As originally written, only about three sailing terms were in the book. But then I met a charming Swedish couple, who told me of their embarrassment when sailing. Though they spoke fluent English, they only knew the sailing terms in Swedish. They felt like neophytes, even though they'd sailed in extreme enough conditions that they had to pour sea water on the "ropes" to thaw

them. That encounter, and my editor's urging, resulted in the inclusion of normal sailing terminology. My advice is: do not spend a minute memorizing. You will learn the terms as you sail. When you handle a line, learn its name, or not, as you choose, and in your own time.

Sailing involves aerodynamics. That shouldn't intimidate. Even a bird-brain just a few weeks old can learn to fly. The parent birds teach by intuition, and their fledglings learn the same way.

Are these birds flying, or sailing their nest with an upper wing as a sail, and the lower as a *keel* and *rudders*? Both sailing and flying have similarities, but sailing is much easier than flying. The book that will teach you to fly safely, today, will probably never be written. If young birds can fly, you can sail.

Birds sense the wind on their feathers. You cannot teach a bird to fly by discussing wing loading, Bernoulli's equation, or wind speeds and direction. You can teach a person to sail that way, but there is an easier way. We can

(Drawing by Clare Rosean)

observe that airflow on our sails and make the sails work for us.

Sails work simply by affecting the airflow around them. Later, in Appendix F, I explain how sails generate motion from the airflow around them. Detailed information on how they work is not needed to sail today, but it will help you increase your skills over time.

The book is organized to get you out on the water today. There is a lot to cover in your first day of sailing.

You will first learn to rig your boat. Figure 1.1 in the chapter "Today, Day One" is a draw-ing of a rigged sailboat, naming the parts of the boat, but that is just to clarify some of the text. Before you sail you will be taught the basics of safe conduct on the water. Then, you will learn to launch the boat, or sail from its dock. The key issue, adjusting the sails so the boat will move at your command, is as simple as can be. It is easier than flying a kite. You have steered before, so learning to avoid other boats, and return to the dock or beach, is not much different from any driving or bicycling you have already done. At the end of the sail, you will learn to fold the sails and stow gear. If you are sailing a larger boat, the big boat will make additional demands on you; these issues are covered as well. If you are sailing with an experienced person, you might only need to learn safety afloat, and to hoist and adjust the sails. In any case, more detailed subjects, unessential for your first day, are left for the following days.

WHY LEARN TO SAIL?

Why learn to sail? Sailing opens the other two-thirds of the world to you: all the earth's waters. Sailing can be anything you want it to be: athletic or leisurely, adventurous or sedentary, challenging or relaxing, a solitary or

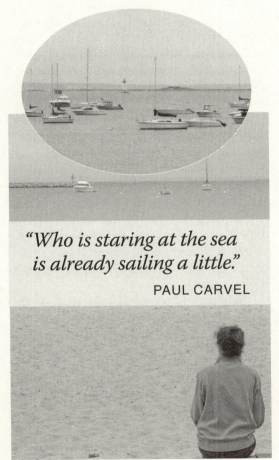

"Who is staring at the sea is already sailing a little."

PAUL CARVEL

"The pessimist says the winds are bad.

The optimist says the winds will change.

The realist adjusts the sails."

WILLIAM ARTHUR WARD

group activity. You can leave "it" all behind, or take it all with you. You can sail for next to nothing, or choose to spend a fortune. The scenery can be spectacular. A lucky few can afford waterfront homes. For a fraction of a waterfront home's cost, you can sail your own waterfront home, moving it wherever and whenever you choose. You can enjoy hours, days, a vacation, or even live aboard. It is all your choice. You can enjoy other hobbies or sports while aboard: fishing and cooking, photography, and scuba diving are some of the most obvious examples.

In 2006, a blind sailor named Alison Dunn completed a solo circumnavigation of the Isle of Wight. In 1989, Howard Rice completed a well-documented rounding of Chile's notorious Cape Horn in a 15-foot folding sailing kayak. Bill Pinkney of Chicago's Belmont Yacht Club became the first African-American to sail solo around the world. These are extreme examples, but proof that people of both sexes; all ages; all races and colors; and all degrees of health, capacity, and fitness can enjoy sailing, and your boat doesn't have to cost a lot.

Sailing is the most rational activity I engage in. It is environmentally sustainable. The sea does not lie. The winds do not deceive. A half hour into the lake, my troubles are two miles west and receding. All that matters is the wind, the sails, the boat, and the scenery.

Yes, you can be both a realist and a sailor. *Today!*

You, the reader, must challenge yourself to continue to learn more and more. This book doesn't attempt to cover every detail about your boat or your sailing waters. It will get you started quickly and well. Your adventure is yours to discover.

Why wait? Let's get started. Just take this book, and add some water. **Today.**

LET'S SAIL TODAY!

> *"Twenty years from now, you'll be more disappointed by the things you didn't do than by the ones you did do. So throw off the bowlines. Sail away from the safe harbor. Catch the trade winds in your sails. Explore. Dream. Discover."*
>
> MARK TWAIN

The weather is beautiful. Do you have a better idea for a fun day in the sun? You do not have an excuse not to learn to sail. Do not say, "I don't know how." Do not say, "I do not have a boat." Or, "I'm afraid." Or any other excuse.

You will know how to sail a boat safely today by the end of the first chapter. You can probably get a boat ride for free. You could buy one for surprisingly little money. Sailing is one of the safest sports around. You will not drown. In the entire year 2014, the official statistics show a total of two drowning deaths of sailors wearing life vests, including all types of sailboats and all U.S. waters. In the first two months of the summer of 2014, at least four times that many beachgoers drowned in Lake Michigan alone. These statistics are typical of every year.

Modern sailboats, properly maintained, do not sink. Fiberglass doesn't leak; fiberglass boats do not just break up except in hurricanes or when smashed on rocks. It's easy to maintain your boat and to avoid hazards. Hurricanes are forecast accurately enough to avoid them. Rocks aren't floating around looking for sailboats to smash; they are charted and

(Photo courtesy of Dan Caplan Photography)

easily avoided. Modern life jackets will keep you afloat for days if need be and can turn an unconscious person face up. A modern sailboat can sail *upwind* well, so you will not be blown out to sea. Larger modern sailboats are usually designed so that they do not capsize, except in the most extreme conditions of wind and waves. Smaller sailboats, which can capsize, can be designed to pop right back up, dry and ready for more fun. It can be so much

PREVENT SEASICKNESS

Seasickness is related to a difference in how your eyes and inner ear perceive movement. Remain on deck, get the fresh air, and keep watching the horizon. Drugless methods of prevention include wrist bands and electrical stimulation devices. Avoid alcohol and greasy foods before and while sailing. Do not go hungry. Hunger pangs can stimulate a feeling of seasickness. Saltines, ginger, ginger ale, or cola drinks will help prevent it. Dramamine and Bonine, antihistamines that can cause drowsiness, are available without a prescription. Sturgeron and Scopalamine are prescription only. The former is not available in the United States. Try any drugs on land first to get familiar with their possible side effects before using while boating.

DON'T LET FEAR KEEP YOU OFF THE WATER

It is common to have a fear of unfamiliar forms of transportation. Many are afraid of flying, some of driving. Sailing is one of the safest activities in existence. The feeling of the boat tilting, called heeling, is unfamiliar; its unfamiliarity is mistaken for danger. The fact that the boat is heeling even 20 degrees does not mean that, even in a huge gust, the boat will capsize. If it is a keelboat, the more the boat heels the more the keel's weight will keep the boat from capsizing, and the more the boat heels, the less the sails are able to push it over. It all cancels out. If it is a boat without a heavy keel, the crew just leans out over the water to balance the boat. Also, the sails can be let out to stop or reduce the tilt.

If you are not involved in a race, and you are uncomfortable with the amount the boat is heeling, say so and ask if you yourself could hold the mainsheet and control the amount of heel. You will be surprised how quickly you get comfortable with a steep angle of heel if you can control it or see how easily it is controlled.

Wear a proper and comfortable life vest. There are very few instances of drowning victims wearing life vests. If it is comfortable, you will be more likely to wear it.

fun to capsize a small sailboat that it is often done intentionally on hot days. And there are remedies for seasickness.

You will be safe.

You can learn to sail easily and quickly.

You can sail today!

Free boat rides are available to everyone who looks. Sure, how you look can help in every sense. But there are free rides available, even if you do not have a friend with a boat.

Check the bulletin board of your local yacht club. Look for a posting for a race boat needing a crew, or post your own "crew available" note. Ask around the local docks on race days. Find racing fleets on the Internet. Racing fleets and yacht clubs' web pages often include

(Drawing by Christopher Hoyt)

listings of boats needing crew. Or, there may be notes posted on their bulletin boards in the club. Be honest about your limited qualifications; novice crew are frequently acceptable. Some races are very casual; those particularly welcome the unskilled. You can learn all you need to be valued aboard by reading and understanding this book. For many races, on many boats, understanding "Day One" will be enough to earn repeated rides. Often, *spinnakers* are not used, or other crew may be aboard to handle that. See Appendix C to learn spinnaker handling. Racing is a great way to develop sailing skills.

Check the Internet for sailing clubs. Your community, your park district, or your local college or university may have one. Some of these have small membership fees and offer instruction as well.

Inexpensive introductory lessons are available through for-profit companies. Once you have learned to their satisfaction, you can rent a yacht from them.

Some instruction combines a vacation with the lessons. Some of these options are intended to have the student achieve certification for a bare-boat charter. Or you can contact a charter company for a boat with captain and just join in and learn as you vacation.

Many resorts offer sailing lessons; some are all-inclusive resorts that might not charge an additional fee for the lesson(s). Inquire in advance; confirm it in writing.

You can buy a boat on a time-share, as on a vacation property. Time-shares on boats usually allow you to pick a certain allotment of days. Some issue a number of "credits," which

THERE IS A STEREOTYPE OF YACHT CLUBS

There may be some clubs that approximate that stereotype of snobiness. For every such club, there are countless others that are inclusive and welcoming. The club I am a member of has a past commodore, an African American, as its only life member and has had commodores male, female, gay and straight, married or single. These are private clubs, so ask permission to enter in order to post a "crew available" note.

you may use whenever a boat is available, with weekdays costing fewer credits than weekends or evenings.

Go to a boat show. You will find sources of instruction, charters, rentals, and new and used boats. Something in your price range to suit your needs will be available.

Do not let the unfamiliar overwhelm you. You already know most of what you have to do. You already know how to steer. You've steered a car, a bicycle, an uncooperative grocery cart, a stroller, a lawn mower, or wheelbarrow. You know how to balance; how to walk on an uneven surface. You have perhaps used ropes. You have used levers and cranks when bicycling. You know something about water safety. So let us begin.

1 YOUR FIRST SAILING ADVENTURE

> *"The secret of getting ahead is getting started. The secret of getting started is breaking your complex overwhelming tasks into small manageable tasks, and then starting on the first one."*
>
> MARK TWAIN

Mark Twain was right. But with sailing there are no tasks. There are fun steps. We will break down learning to sail today into seven steps for your first day, and twenty-one steps in all. The steps are fewer, and simpler, if you learn on a small sailboat, and fewer still to start sailing as a crew member. Welcome! Sail today! Sail often!

THE FIRST STEP: A BRIEF OVERVIEW

Your first sailing adventure will be safe, fun, and a bit challenging. Be sure of all of the following:

- ☑ Have this book, and a thorough understanding of Day One.
- ☑ Understand basic safety.
- ☑ As a beginner, sail in daylight only.
- ☑ Have suitable weather:

- ◆ No large waves.
- ◆ Wind speed 5 to 12 mph. Become aware of the wind speed and direction at all times, because it will frequently change. Less wind is okay, but it will be harder to sail.
- ◆ Wind blowing along or toward shore, not blowing away from shore.
- ◆ Have a device to help you see where the wind is coming from. If there isn't a pointer at the top of the mast, just tie some lightweight cloth strips (*telltales*) or yarn to vertical wires on the boat. In case of very light winds, bring a bottle of children's soap bubble solution. Watching the bubbles float away will tell you about the local winds.
- ◆ Know of any current or tides.
- ◆ Have a weather radio.

☑ Have a map (*chart*) of your sailing territory.
☑ Know the location of any shallow water or obstructions in the vicinity. It is a very good idea to discuss this with a local sailor.
☑ Recognize the type of buoys marking the channel. Make a note of them; be able to follow the proper route in and out of the harbor. You could photograph the channel, its markings, and entrance with a digital camera as you are departing, to use as a reference for your return.
☑ Wear a *life vest*.
☑ Have a sailboat in good condition with the mast and rigging proper. (Have someone knowledgeable check it out, or examine it as described in Day Four.)
☑ Have food and water for twice the time you anticipate being out on the water.
☑ Have clothing that will keep you warm and dry. Remember, even a sunny day can turn cold, and you will be much colder if

wet from rain or spray. Layers are the key to comfort.
☑ Have a bailing bucket and a sponge. Tie the bucket to the boat.
☑ If on a larger boat, everyone on board should know:
- ◆ The location of and how to operate the marine radio and the fire extinguishers.
- ◆ How to operate the engine.
- ◆ How to lower and *hoist* the anchor. (For today, just know how to tie it to the boat and drop it in the water, using a length of line about seven times the depth of the water. There may be machinery—called a *windlass*—to operate it, or you may need to find it below decks, tie its rope to a cleat, and lower it into the water.)
- ◆ How to raise (hoist) and lower (*douse*) the sails.
- ◆ How to tie and untie the boat at the dock.
- ◆ The location of the life vests.
- ◆ The location of the first-aid kit.
- ◆ The location of the pumps and bailing bucket.

It is recommended that you have a sailing partner with some experience.

Begin on a small sailboat. As you can see from the list, that makes beginning easier. If you must learn on a larger boat, the additional things you must learn are covered in later sections. I'll help you break down all the tasks for your first day sailing into small, easily followed steps.

With the winds blowing onshore or along the shore, if all else fails, you will not be blown out to sea. You will learn to rig, sail, and steer the boat and learn basic safety. Have other boats around to help you out in case you need it.

Small sailboats are often called *dinghies*. There are many advantages to learning on a dinghy: you can practice a bit right on the sand at the beach; they are more responsive, so you immediately see the effects of your actions; they can be far less expensive to buy and maintain; you can store them in your garage for free; and they are available at many resorts, sometimes without charge. If you learn on a boat without a heavy keel, such as a dinghy, you must either also learn how to right the boat after a capsize or have someone knowledgeable aboard.

THE SECOND STEP: PREPARE YOUR BOAT

Set your dinghy on land near the water, on the beach or pier. Rig it on shore, if possible. If your boat is in the water, stay for now at the pier or mooring.

The *hull* and the *rigging* make up the boat. The hull is the body of the boat, which will float you and support the rigging. The rigging includes all the parts that handle the sails: the mast, its supporting wires (if any), the *boom* (which holds the bottom of the mainsail), and various sail controls. The hull has a rudder at the rear to steer the boat, and a *centerboard*, *daggerboard*, or *keel* just forward of the center of the boat, which keeps the boat from sliding across the water and keeps it going in the intended direction. Absent the keel, centerboard, or daggerboard, sailing is somewhat like riding a unicycle instead of a bicycle. The two wheels work together in a bicycle to help you travel in the intended direction. The keel and rudder work together similarly. A keel can incorporate a lot of ballast to counterbalance the sideways tilting caused by the sails.

Hull preparation

The rudder and centerboard or daggerboard must be inserted and attached (connected with bungee cords or their own fittings). They must be left retracted and cannot be lowered to stick out of the bottom until after launching.

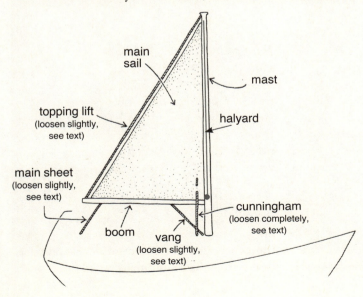

main sail

mast

topping lift
(loosen slightly, see text)

halyard

main sheet
(loosen slightly, see text)

boom

vang
(loosen slightly, see text)

cunningham
(loosen completely, see text)

Figure 1.1. (Drawing by Christopher Hoyt)

7

Plugs must be securely inserted in any drain holes. Many boats have keels that are permanently attached; some can be raised and lowered. Regardless, the rule for now is to lower any rudder, centerboard, daggerboard, or "retractable" keel as soon as the water level permits, secure it in its fully down position, and leave it that way until and unless you reach water too shallow to permit this.

Rigging preparation

The mast, boom, and sails get connected. This varies from boat to boat. What boat will you learn on?

I've sailed a Laser a Sunfish, and a Flying Junior more often than other dinghies. These three boats, together with the tiny Optimist for the very young and lightweight crowd, are representative of the most common types of dinghies. The Laser is a high-performance boat, but in light winds (only!) it can be a beginner's boat. The problem with the Laser as a beginner's boat is that its instability can be frustrating and tiring. A Laser is usually left unrigged, because rigging is so simple, and the sail cannot be lowered with the mast in place.

If you have the option, and warm water to sail on, the Sunfish is an excellent first boat. The Sunfish is stable, responsive, and capable of good

Figure 1.2. **An Optimist dinghy. The young skipper is setting the centerboard.**

performance. A Sunfish is often left rigged, because the sail can be lowered with the mast up. A Flying Junior is a two-person boat, with two sails, so you can have a more experienced person aboard as you learn. A Flying Junior is often left with the mast up, because the rigging involves wires that go from the boat to the top of the mast and hold the mast in place. Because the Optimist is for children weighing under about 90 pounds, wherever you might find one, you likely will find an adult to rig one. I've never sailed an "Opti," but it is said that 80 percent of the medal winners at the 2012 Olympics learned on one. Robert Perry, one of the top sailboat designers, still shoehorns his six-foot-plus frame into an eight-foot El Toro dinghy.

I learned on small scows (a scow is a dinghy with a nearly flat bottom and rounded bow). If you can find a 12-foot beginner's scow, such as a Bat, a Hawk, or a Butterfly, you will find a stable yet thrilling platform to sail on. Many people will start out on whatever boat they can obtain economically. That's okay, but do spend a lot of time on a responsive dinghy. Do not start with a boat that has a *trapeze*.

Catamarans are okay, but they won't teach you essentials of balance, nor are they generally good for learning upwind sailing. A smaller high-performance *keelboat* (the Colgate 26, Etchells, J 22, J 24, Soling, Sonar, and Star are some examples) is okay to learn on. They are more stable

Figure 1.3.
An example of yards and the complex rigging on a tall ship.

and dry than the dinghies, yet responsive enough to teach the effects of sail trim. They also provide plenty of room for an experienced sailor to join you. Be sure the boat has good sails. Sails that are stretched out from overuse will interfere with your learning proper sail trim.

When rigging, refer to the manual or drawings of your own particular boat. Following is a description of rigging a Laser. A Laser has two mast sections. The thicker one is at the bottom. Assemble the two sections. Fit the mast into the sail's sleeve, starting with the top of the mast at the bottom of the sail, and slide it in until the sail is completely on and pulled down the mast as far as it will go. Place the mast in the mast *step*, which in this case is a hole. Place the boom in its *fitting*, a rod that will stick into the boom. Attach the sail control lines, starting with the *outhaul*, and continuing with the *clew* tie down, the *mainsheet*, the *vang*, and *cunningham*.

Ropes aren't called ropes on boats. Instead, they are called either *halyards*, which raise sails (think of the "yards" on tall ships, and a rope to haul it up as a "haul yard"); *sheets* (think of a prisoner making a rope from bed sheets), which are the principle controls for sails; *rodes*, which are anchor ropes; or lines, which are all other ropes. The sheet starts at a figure-eight knot on one end of the rope (I'll teach that), goes through the *traveler*'s block (pulley), then goes through several blocks on the boom and leads to a ratchet block in the hull. Be sure to listen for and feel the ratcheting of the block as you pull the mainsheet in before setting off. The *tiller* gets slipped underneath the back portion of the traveler rope, but above the front. A metal clip on the *stern* holds the rudder in place. A supplemental rope so the rudder cannot be lost is recommended.

The daggerboard is lowered into place. It should be secured with a bungee cord or rope to keep it from sliding off the boat when it is lifted out. A hiking strap runs from the front of the small cockpit (really a footwell) to the rear. It needs to be loose enough to get your feet under but tight enough to keep you in position. The Laser is the simplest boat to rig. The Sunfish adds a halyard (a rope going to the top of the mast to haul the sail up) to the mix. The Flying Junior adds a second halyard and three wires holding the mast (*shrouds* and a *stay*). The last couple times I went sailing on friends' Lasers, both had forgotten the clew tie-down. I watched an Internet video on rigging a Sunfish. No mention was made of the drain plug, and the instructor set the mast on a narrow dock as he worked. The mast could have rolled off, a costly error. Personal instruction on rigging your particular boat is advised. As you are shown how to rig your particular boat, ask questions. Be sure every rope is in place and properly set and all hardware is secured. Watch for missing cotter pins and retaining rings, as well as unplugged holes.

Knots

There will be two types of knots to learn today, and a third, the *Bowline* hitch, if you are on a larger boat. Each of these three knots starts in exactly the same way. The first two knots are the *Stopper Knot* and the *Cleat Hitch*. The Stopper Knot is easy. The Cleat Hitch is a snap. The Bowline is . . . not so much.

It helps to think of the rope as having a working part and a main part. We will use those terms. More nautically appropriate terms are "free part" (working) and "standing part" (main).

Figure 1.4. To begin the Stopper Knot, lay the line on top of itself as shown above. You have just laid the working part on top of the main part. To simplify learning, we will begin with a turn to the left, or counter-clockwise, forming a loop, to begin tying all four knots in this book.

Figure 1.5. After forming the loop, pass the working part underneath the main part of the rope.

STOPPER KNOT. The Stopper Knot keeps the lines from running past the blocks so they stay in reach.

When do I use the Stopper Knot? The Stopper Knot is used any time you want to be sure a line doesn't run free. It is tied at the end of sheets, halyards, and other lines. It fattens up the end to prevent it from running past turning blocks or other small openings, so the line will stay within reach of the crew.

CLEAT HITCH. The Cleat Hitch is simply a Stopper Knot wrapped around a cleat after a half turn around the cleat.

Figure 1.6. Continue to bring the working part of the line around the main part.

Figure 1.7. Bring the working part through the first loop you formed, creating a figure eight.

Figure 1.8. Cinch it up tight and you are done.

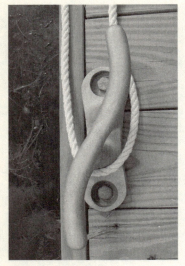

Figure 1.9.

Before starting to tie the Cleat Hitch, first the rope is brought to the farthest vertical surface of the cleat from the boat, as in Figure 1.9. Next, we bring the rope through three-quarters of a turn around the cleat, as shown in Figure 1.10. From then on, the Cleat Hitch is pretty much the Stopper Knot you just learned, tied on a cleat.

Depending on the position of the boat, line and cleat, it may be desirable to tie this as a mirror image to the photos.

In the final steps, the Cleat Hitch is finished by taking the working part of the rope under the horizontal part of the cleat and then back over the horizontal part of the cleat (see Figure 1.11). The working part then is led under the part of the rope it crosses and the knot is then cinched up tightly (see Figure 1.12).

When do I use the Cleat Hitch? The Cleat Hitch is used any time you tie a line to a cleat. It is used for mooring to a pier.

Figure 1.10. Bring the rope around the vertical part and pull it over the horizontal part at an angle. This is the now-familiar first counter-clockwise turn to the left.

Figure 1.11. Continue around. Begin to form a figure eight.

Figure 1.12. Finish the figure eight, and cinch it up tight.

Many boats have such cleats to tie sheets and halyards. Properly tied, and protected from chafing (frictional wear), the knot will last as long as the rope does.

THE THIRD STEP: LEARNING BASIC SAFETY

Boats are way safer than in Van Gogh's day. You will learn to be safe aboard today!

Before you get aboard

1. Have nothing in your hands. Anything you bring should first be placed in the boat before you get aboard. To hand anything to someone aboard, have your hand, the object, and the recipient's hand fully over the boat, so important things will not be dropped into the water. The natural tendency to reach toward each other can mean that your hands are over the water as you hand over the item. Eventually, you will drop something.
2. See where you should step and what strong point you should hold onto as you step from the dock to the boat.
3. If getting into a very small boat, such as a dinghy, step to the center of the boat and sit quickly. Be sure you do not pull it over with your hands or flip it over with your weight as you get in.
4. Do not pause with one foot on the boat, the other on the dock. This is dangerous.

Once you are all aboard

1. Secure everything you bring aboard. The bailing bucket should be tied to the boat with a line long enough to use the bailer while it is tied to the boat.
2. Take a look at the overall condition of the boat. Look for frayed wires holding up the mast, and missing or damaged cotter pins.
3. Always remember to keep your hands safe—do not let them get caught on a rope or a piece of hardware on the boat.
4. Always remember to keep your footing. Hold onto something whenever you are standing or walking on the deck.
5. If you did not already learn, see what ropes (halyards) raise the sail(s), and where they are connected. At the end of the day, or

> "*The fishermen know the sea [has dangers] but they have never found these dangers sufficient reason for remaining ashore.*"
>
> VINCENT VAN GOGH

in an emergency, or to *reef* the main (partially lowering it, as can be done in larger boats), the sails will be lowered by reversing the procedure used to raise them.

6. If the boat is turning or sails are being adjusted, be sure you aren't hit hard by the sails or anything attached to them, like the boom.

7. Stay with the boat in any emergency. Even if the boat is sinking, stay with the boat until it is just about to slip beneath the waves, then remain right next to it until it is gone. Small boats will not have enough suction to pull you under. Only in the event a fire forces you off should you leave a floating boat, and even then stay just far enough away to not get burned. Do not attempt to swim to shore.

Safe is fun. Thinking you may die: not so much. Some of the above rules are self-explanatory. Others merit the following further discussion. There are safe things, and dangerous things, which can seem similar.

You are about to go sailing. You have checked the weather report, and no storms are predicted. The winds are not excessive (which depends on the boat and the skill of all aboard). For beginners, I recommend a maximum of 12 mph winds.

Get aboard safely as described above. Once aboard, get an overview of the condition of the boat, the handholds and lines, and estimate the crew's seating positions. Look around for tripping and falling hazards. Look where portholes and hatches are; you may need to close them in a hurry, and you should not stand on a hatch. The latches on these vary, but are usually obvious. When they are closed, they should be latched tight.

Stay aboard the boat

To keep you from falling off, do not step around without secure footing and a handhold. Look out for ropes, and do not walk on ropes or sails. If you step on any, it is almost like stepping on

OR

Figure 1.13. They look similar, but one is a dangerous cheetah, and the other is a pet. (Drawing by Christopher Hoyt)

ball bearings. Learn to walk on the high side of a tilted (*heeled*) boat; it is safer because you have more chance to grip something if you fall. Do not go between a sail and the edge of the boat. If the sail is let out, or the rope parts, the sail can sweep you overboard. Avoid loaded hardware, the blocks (pulleys) and other sail-control hardware in use. Jewelry can get caught or lost; put it away. Put your cell phone and camera in a waterproof bag, and secure the bag in the boat or your pocket. Remember at all times, and especially as you move about, the boat can shift without warning. Never pee overboard!

Sailing in fair weather

Here the dangers are from failure to keep a proper look-out, failure to navigate properly and getting stuck aground (or worse), sunburn, and swimming. Swimming near other boats, or in a harbor, is ill-advised. An electrical problem aboard even one boat can electrocute a swimmer. An inattentive boater can run you down.

It is shockingly, and sometimes fatally, difficult to climb back aboard a boat from the water. One weekend as I was working on this book (the second weekend of August 2010), in two separate incidents six people died of drowning or hypothermia, and five children were left drifting and bawling in a reservoir after watching all the adults perish. All this occurred in good weather. Have I gotten your attention?

In neither case were the swimmers able to climb back aboard. In one of the cases, the boat drifted away. Only one of the six dead had a flotation device, and reports say he only had one arm through it. No throwable devices were used.

I hope my readers will never place themselves in that situation. If swimming is planned, first anchor the boat. Be sure the anchor is holding securely. Turn off any and all high-voltage current. Then, set out the swim ladder. Secure it to the boat.

Shut the engine off. Deploy a number of lines, one end tied to the boat, the other tied to a life vest in a way that allows a swimmer to don it if needed. Yes, it is better to wear it at all times, but I know that sometimes will not happen. Be sure a throwable device is available. At least one person who can operate the boat and the radio should remain on the boat at all times. He or she can join in the fun as soon as the first person returns. Have only one crew in the water at first. Can that crew climb back aboard unassisted? If not, consider that if everyone is in the water, no one can get out. Re-rig your ladder until you are certain a tired swimmer can get aboard unaided.

Hypothermia can occur even in warmish waters. Be sure you can recognize the signs of it.

Life vests

Wear one! It is good practice for all crew on deck, including those in a recessed cockpit, to wear a life vest at all times. It does no good if not worn. It should be U.S. Coast Guard approved. There are those who choose to wear a European life vest, which is not Coast Guard approved, but you should be able to find a comfortable, approved life vest. With minimal maintenance it will remain in good condition. A throwable flotation device is also essential on any boat with two or more persons aboard, and one is *required* on any boat over 16 feet long. Preferably it should have a long, lightweight, floating rope attaching it to the boat.

While a good sailing school may mandate the use of their life vests, you may want to purchase your own early on, perhaps even before you set foot on a boat. If you can swim, an inflatable life vest may be your best choice. An inflatable can be so comfortable you hardly know you are wearing it. A comfortable vest is more likely to be worn, so it is more likely to be where you need it. Regardless of the brand or type, try it on before you buy it. Make sure it is comfortable enough to wear for hours and hours in various kinds of weather. Be sure you know how to adjust it, inspect it, inflate it, and maintain it. Everyone aboard should be happy you are wearing a life vest. If not, you are on the wrong boat.

Consider also the following: Inflatables can be manual, or have automatic inflation plus manual options. If the inflatable automatically inflates on contact with water, it can trap you in an overturned cockpit, but it can save you even if you are unconscious. Some inflatables are worn like a belt. Those are the most comfortable types, but note that, when needed, the vest must be pulled out from the belt pack, pulled over your head, and then inflated. I have not seen a belt vest that can be pulled on after inflation, or an automatically inflating belt vest. Foam vests are bulkier, but they are preferable for the non-swimmer. Some types can be very comfortable to wear. If you can get comfortable with a foam vest, use it. The foam vest has a safety advantage over the inflatable but only if it is actually worn. On a boat that gets the sailors wet, such as a dinghy, the automatic inflatable is not an option. On a boat that is capsize prone, such as the Laser, a foam life vest is a much better choice. Flotation jackets ("float coats") combine a life vest with a foul weather jacket. In cooler weather, these can provide safety, comfort, and warmth.

Other gear for the beginner

Your gear as a non-owner will generally be only what you wear, together with a good grade of sun block and perhaps insect repellant. Have clothes for all anticipated weather. All layers should be fast-drying. Preferably all outerwear should be of high-tech, breathable, water-repellant material. Your clothing choice should be based upon the water temperature as well as the air temperature. In colder weather, ski-type clothing is great for a beginner sailor; although not designed to keep water out, it tends to be water-resistant and protect against spray (polypropylene and fleece materials keep you warm, absorb little water, and dry quickly). Several thin layers are better than one heavy one. Waterproof socks and shoes are available. Shoes that give traction on a wet deck are essential. They must have a white or very light-colored sole to avoid marring the deck. For a first few rides, any white-soled athletic shoes will do. Paul A. Sperry, the inventor of the ubiquitous boat shoe, originally utilized ordinary athletic shoes. He used a razor blade to cut tread grooves like tires have in his gym shoes. For fresh water, leather or canvas shoes will do, but in salt water, leather shoes can pick up a horrible smell.

Figure 1.14. (Drawing by Christopher Hoyt)

Sail handling is easier and safer with gloves. At this point, the cheapest pair to fit you will be fine, unless cold weather is a factor. Your boat may or may not have extras on board and may or may not have a size that fits you. Hardware-store gloves will be cheap, are better than none, and can be used for other jobs.

If you are just going on a short ride, especially in daytime, signaling gear can consist of a simple flat-shaped marine whistle. (The kind referees use with the rounded part and little balls inside does not work when wet.) Tuck it in somewhere; the longer the lanyard, the greater chance of it catching on something and choking you or breaking off. Of course, the better safety option at night is a waterproof rescue light together with the whistle, but your flash camera or smartphone, protected with a waterproof cover or in a bag, can save your life. Remember to flash it at any potential rescue boat, and flash it at least two times as quickly as possible. It is tough for people to determine just where in the sea a single flash came from. As an added benefit, you can wind up with great pictures. A small mirror can be used as a signal, especially in daylight. Try to aim the sun's reflection at a potential rescuer.

Additional safety issues on larger boats

1. Close all hatches and doors, and close off the cabin from the cockpit. Later, as you gain experience, you can learn what ventilation is safe in what conditions.
2. Note the location of the fire extinguishers. See how they work. Fires aboard are rare. Fire extinguishers have a pin to prevent accidental use. To use, the pin must be pulled completely out. Aim the extinguisher at the base, not the top, of the flames. Squeeze the trigger and sweep across the burning area. Never use water on a gas or electrical fire. Shut off all fuel and electricity to help stop such fires.
3. Note the location of the ship-to-shore radio. Note the on/off switch and the channel selector. The radio should be turned on and set to channel 16 whenever you are sailing. In an emergency, you will make sure it is turned on and set on channel 16 with the volume loud. Press the microphone button (almost always on the left side), and describe in clear terms the nature of your emergency (e.g., medical emergency: excessive bleeding); the name and a brief description of your boat (e.g., *Raven*, a 30-foot, off-white, masthead *sloop*); and your location as best you can describe it. Release the microphone button when you are done speaking, or you will not hear any reply. More details are in Day Three.

4. Note the location of the GPS. Learn at least how to operate the crew overboard (COB, POB, "person overboard," or MOB, "man overboard") button, and how to use the GPS to return to the harbor. (Later you will learn techniques to find the harbor in the absence of a GPS.)

5. Use a harness and tether on a keelboat (not a dinghy), especially at night or in rough weather. Consider a tether with two attachment points plus a third connecting to your harness, so that as you move about you can hook one part in before releasing the other part. Make sure the tether's connections, especially the one on the harness/your side, release easily when intended, even under strain and while wearing your sailing gloves, and do not release except when intended. The tether should be set so you cannot fall off. It is far less effective at keeping you safely close to the boat if you should fall overboard. On centerboard boats and dinghies, tethers are not used, because a tether can trap you underneath an overturned boat.

6. Control all halyards. When readying or dousing a sail, if you let go of an unattached halyard, it will be difficult to reach it again as it sways from the mast top in the waves and breeze.

7. Make sure no ropes are dragging in the water. If a rope should wrap around the propeller, you will have a problem.

8. Know how to anchor the boat in an emergency. Proper anchoring will be taught another day. For today, if an emergency occurs, and the boat cannot be maneuvered, you can lower an anchor. Estimate how deep the bottom is. See how much line is used to get the anchor to touch bottom. In calm conditions, let out at least three times that depth of line. Seven times the depth is preferable.

THE FOURTH STEP:
CONNECT THE SAILS PROPERLY

1. Attach the halyard to the sail. The halyard attaches to the sail with a shackle. Each sail has a halyard, excepting some dinghies.

2. The mainsail connects to the boom at the front and back, and sometimes along the length of the boom. If you feel a very thick bottom edge of the mainsail, as though there is a rope inside the bottom edge, that is the signal that the mainsail gets fed through the slot in the top of the boom.

3. Every sail has at least one sheet and *jibs* (the sail in front of the mast), usually two. A mainsheet connects the boom to the hull. A jib sheet is connected to the bottom rear of the sail (the *clew*), usually using a bowline. Sheets must be connected properly to the sail and the boat before the sails are raised. Instructions on *bowlines* are in Day Three, the fourteenth step.

4. The front of the mainsail connects to the mast. The mainsail may have a rope sewn in its front. This gets fed into the slot as the mainsail is hoisted. Or the main may have fittings to connect to the mast. The Sunfish and Laser, two popular dinghies, have a different system, previously discussed.

Figure 1.15. Often halyards are attached to sails with a special fitting called a shackle. The sailor in this photo has just clipped a halyard to the mainsail. The halyard is used to lift the sail up to the top of the mast. The shackle is attached to a reinforced top tip of the sail called a *headboard,* the dark triangular shape in the figure. This shackle has a "captive pin." The zone for the captive pin where it is locked in securely is marked by ridges.

Another common type of shackle is shown in Figure 1.16.

A jib may often be attached to a taut wire (forestay) running from the bow to the mast by clips called *hanks*. See Figure 1.17.

The jib hanks have a piston that is retracted so the hank can be attached to the wire forestay. Connect the bottom front of the sail to a *tack* fitting, which is usually located on the deck immediately behind the forestay. Clip each hank in its turn to the forestay, starting from the sail's bottom. The hanks should all face the same direction, as in the photo. Or, the front of the sail might have a rope sewn in to feed into a track on the forestay.

For a discussion of jib furlers and winches see Day Three, the fifteenth step.

The halyards should be easy enough to identify. The main halyard goes to the top of the mast and comes down the rear of the mast to connect to the sail with a shackle. There may also be a *topping lift*, which looks similar, but is attached to the rear of the boom. The jib halyard is at the front of the mast and goes to the top of the forestay. Many boats feature halyards run through the mast to reduce air friction. Marine line often has flecks of color in addition to its base color. This helps distinguish various lines from one another. ("Get the halyard and tighten it. It's the blue one with the white flecks.") See Figure 1.18.

Here's a safety tip: The ropes held in these cleats may be under extreme tension. Before releasing the cleat, take a wrap of the free part

Figure 1.17. Hanks and jib

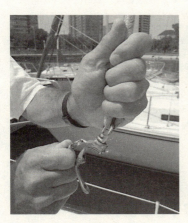

Figure 1.16. The shackle is open and ready to attach to the sail and close. It is essential the pin is secured in the shackle. If it is the screw-in type, twist it securely. Pliers, or a shackle blade on a marine knife, will give you leverage to secure it. If it is a plunger type, be sure the pin goes all the way in. For longer voyages, seizing wire can be used to secure it.

Figure 1.18. There will be some form of cleat to hold the halyard in place.

Figure 1.19. Cleats may be used to hold halyards, sheets, mooring lines, and anchor rodes in place. Cleats for sheets are more likely to be jam or clam cleats, or on larger boats sheets may be held in place by self-tailing winches. In this photo, the three cleats on the left are rope clutches. With the lever down as in the photo, the line can be pulled inwards from the clutch (toward the bottom of the photo) but will not go in the opposite direction unless the lever is lifted. On the right is a jam cleat. The rope is placed in the jam cleat and tensioned by pulling it outwards, causing the rope to sink into the jam cleat. The wire at the back of the jam cleat can be placed over the line, reducing the chance of accidentally removing the line from the cleat.

(working part) of the rope around a winch to take some of the load off and prevent an accident.

THE FIFTH STEP: PRACTICE AT THE DOCK OR ON THE BEACH

The hull and rigging are ready, and you have learned basic safety. So you and the boat are now ready to learn to sail today. Let us begin, if at all possible, while still on shore.

Set the boat on the beach or pier, with the rudder and centerboard or daggerboard still retracted. Put your life jacket on now. If you are on a pier, it will help keep you safe in case you fall off. Even if there is no danger of falling into the water, it is a good idea to get used to maneuvering about the boat while wearing one. Try to avoid scratching the hull. Place beach towels under it to prevent scratches. Figure out the wind direction, and draw a line pointing in the direction of the wind. Make sure any people nearby will not get hit by the boat if it is flipped on its side.

Hoist the sails

Refer to the drawing identifying lines at the beginning of the chapter.

1. To raise or lower the sails, you just pull tight or release the halyard, which is first attached to the top of the sail. Raise it as high as it will go. When it can go no further, pull on it moderately hard to tension it. You will learn another day when and why the tension is changed. As you raise the sails, look up to be sure the sail doesn't snag on something. If the sail is large you will need a winch to pull on the rope. Then secure the halyard on its cleat or rope clutch. Lowering the sail may require that the sail be pulled down as the line is eased.
2. The first sail you will most likely raise is the mainsail. The mainsail may have a number of lines attached to it. Locate the mainsheet, connecting the boom to the hull, thereby controlling the main sail. Loosen it a bit before raising the sail. If tight, you will be pulling against it when you hoist the mainsail. There may also be a line extending from near the middle of the boom to near the bottom of the mast (a *vang*). Loosen that as well for the same reason. Refer to the drawing of boat parts in Day One, Figure 1.1.
3. It is more difficult to raise sails if they are pressed by the wind. Allow each sail to *luff* or flap, pointed into the wind, as it is raised.

If your boat is on the beach, point the boat in the exact direction of the wind. Can you set the sails properly now? No, you cannot. You will have to turn the bow of the boat away from the wind, perhaps 30 degrees from the wind, before you can even get the sails to fill properly. Because of friction while sailing (water and air resistance), the boat must be pointed about 45 degrees from the wind before the boat will be able to overcome the friction of the water and air and move forward well. Turn the boat further and further from the wind, and see how the sail sets. Look for the point at which the sail first fills and forms that airplane wing–like shape. Notice that the sail sets that way at the same angle to the wind regardless of the direction the boat is pointed. You will see the boat might start to tip away from the wind. Counteract that with your weight. Sit toward the edge of the boat the wind is first coming over. This will be the side that is rising as a result of the wind pressure on the sail. In dinghy sailing, the sailors are the only ballast. Lean out as necessary to keep the boat level.

This is called hiking out. There is no keel to keep a dinghy upright. Be very conscious of wind direction and sail trim.

Sail today!

Remember that the centerboard and rudder must be in the full upwards position or removed while the boat sits on dry land. Before launching, see how these are lowered and secured. See how the sheets are controlled. Take a last check of the weather, both using the weather radio and your eyes: look at the cloud shapes and patterns before you leave the dock and from time to time while sailing. Remember, if the clouds start building vertically, or a line of clouds approaches at a low level, it is time to head for safety.

If you are launching in shallow water, from a beach or ramp, it will be necessary to pull the boat out toward deeper water and climb aboard once the boat is in deep enough water to lower the rudder and centerboard about halfway. This should be roughly waist-deep water at most. It may be possible to reach into the boat and lower the rudder and centerboard partially before getting aboard. Look at the mainsail. It will be luffing until it is later pulled in by the sheet. Point the boat in a safe direction (not toward shore, a swimmer, or an obstacle). Next, turn the boat so that the luffing mainsail is aimed not directly at the stern, but at the side or at least the edge of the *transom* (rear panel of the boat). With the sail to one side, climb aboard to the other side and do these steps in this order:

1. If not already done, immediately lower the centerboard partially, without letting it drag on the bottom.
2. If not already done, grab the rudder; lower it partially.
3. Take the tiller and point it straight. Pull in on the mainsheet until the sail just forms its smooth, wing-like shape.

You are sailing! But only for a moment. We will do a capsize drill as close to shore as possible. Then, we will return to our first sailing adventure.

Larger boats

Turn on the marine radio to channel 16 and set the volume and squelch control as advised in your radio manual. For local use, set the squelch control to the point it just eliminates static. Set the weather radio to give storm alerts (you will also listen to the forecasts from time to time, more frequently when the clouds or sea state change). Make sure all dock lines are clear and ready to release. If there is power from shore, turn it off at the dock and unplug the connector at the boat.

Sailing from a dock

Take a look at how the boat is tied to the dock. You will tie it up just like that at the end of the day. You could take a picture to help you restore the lines at the end of the day. If you are in a tidal area, note that your mooring method must account for the rise and fall of the water. Some docks float, so they rise and fall with your boat in the tide. Others have rings that rise and fall on a post.

Get a feel for the steering. Practice turning the rudder all the way over quickly from one side to the other.

Try raising and lowering the sails. Practice until you can raise and lower them as soon as you desire without searching for the correct halyard. Once the sail is up, snug up but do not over tighten any of the lines you loosened in order to raise the sail. Then, try letting the sails out and pulling them in as though you were adjusting for a change in the wind direction.

You need not use the jib today, but try hoisting it and checking it out.

Rehearse the *tack* maneuver while tied to the dock. Tacking is an essential skill covered as the Seventh Step in this chapter. Adjust the tiller or wheel as though you are tacking. Turn it all the way, as far as it will go without forcing it. While turning, reach for the correct lines to let the sail out on one side and pull it in on the other side.

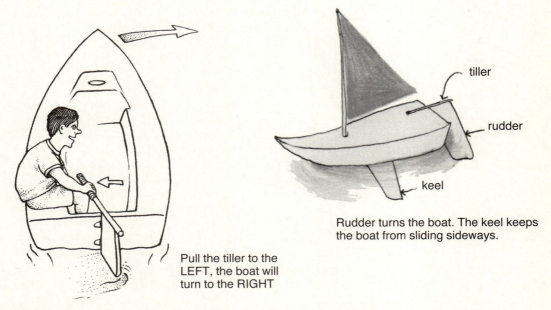

Pull the tiller to the LEFT, the boat will turn to the RIGHT

tiller

rudder

keel

Rudder turns the boat. The keel keeps the boat from sliding sideways.

Figure 1.20. (left drawing by Christopher Hoyt, right drawing by Clare Rosean)

Plan your departure. Make sure there are no boats going by.

1. Use the wind, current, or a good shove to push the bow away from the dock, if there is room to allow that. See if that will put you at a favorable angle to start sailing.
2. Untie all lines except the shortest bow and stern lines; coil and stow them.
3. Untie the bow line and quickly walk back to the stern (in a variation of this, you can take a long line from the bow and hold the boat in to the pier as you walk along the pier, holding the line as tight as necessary. (Because we are doing this in light winds, there is no danger of you being pulled off the pier, but, obviously, if you start to get pulled off, tie the line or let it go.) The bow will start swinging out. Step in the boat.
4. Untie the stern line and throw it on the pier or into the boat.
5. Sheet in and go.

If the wind or current is behind you, the easiest way to get away from the dock is to push the bow away from the dock and let the wind behind you push you along. If the current is pushing you, remember: *you cannot steer unless your boat is moving through, not with, the water.* A current can carry you along, leaving you no steerage. As always, plan ahead.

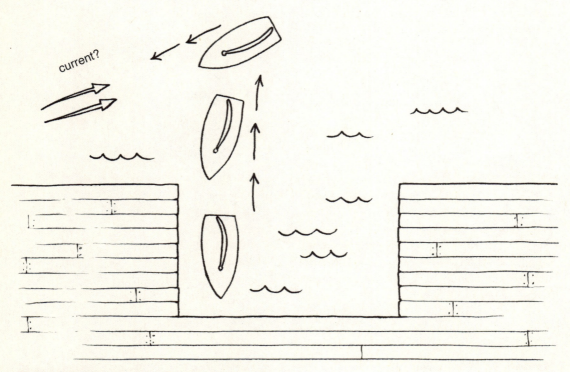

current?

Figure 1.21. (Drawing by Christopher Hoyt)

If your dock is shaped like a U, giving you only one way out, typically your boat will be tied so its bow is pointing in. Backing out will be your only option.

If you have no engine, and the wind will not carry you out of the dock, you must haul the boat away from its confines in the dock. Start with the steps above. Then:

1. Pull the boat into position at the end of the dock.
2. Turn it to face a suitable direction to sail away.
3. Give it a good push away from the dock.
4. Grab the rudder and sheets, and sail away.

Remember that the boat will respond sluggishly to the steering because you are going slowly. Remember, too, that whenever you back up your rudder is particularly exposed to danger. The steering may also be far heavier when you back up than it was at the dock as you practiced. This is because of the shape of the rudder; it is designed to go forward, not backwards (Engine operation is discussed in The Sixteenth Step).

Steer along the channel making no wake, staying toward the right side of the channel, and head to the area you will be sailing in. If you have an engine, you will see it is pushing a cylinder of water backwards. Think about this a moment: if we can send the equivalent weight of air backwards at that speed, the boat will move forward at the same speed. We will do that with the sails. There are additional materials on how to visualize and understand sail trim in Appendix F.

Capsize recovery

Unless you are sailing a Laser, you may never capsize your dinghy. If you do, it is most likely to happen soon, while you are inexperienced. Capsize recovery is an essential safety skill for all dinghy sailors and must be learned on your first day. It can only be practiced in safe places. It is probably too dangerous to practice in the vicinity of docks and other moored vessels. Never enter the water near any power lines, including moored boats with power cords.

Practice capsize recovery close to shore. Try it first in water shallow enough to stand in but deep enough for the keel or centerboard to never touch the bottom, which can damage it or the boat if it hits hard enough. This means you will be close to shore, so make sure no one nearby can be struck by the mast. Capsize the boat intentionally, recover it, and climb aboard. What did you do well, and what needed more attention? Did the cockpit come up dry, or did you need to bail out water? What kept the bucket and other things aboard the capsized boat? Once you are confident in your abilities near shore, rest a while. Then try it in water too deep to touch bottom, with an assistant in another boat nearby equipped with a tow line, just in case.

To recover from a capsize, stand on the centerboard until the boat pops up, which it will. The boat can recapsize. It is less likely to do so if you bring the boat up so the sail is coming up against the wind (the sail starts out to leeward, away from the wind, like a weathervane). So, you must note the wind and align the boat so you can tip it back up by standing on the centerboard with the centerboard more or less facing the direction the wind is coming from.

However, you cannot stand on the centerboard if it has not been fully deployed, slipped up into the boat, floated away, or sunk. That is another reason your centerboard should be secured with some sort of rope, or perhaps a bungee cord, before you start sailing.

The sailor pictured has no daggerboard to stand on to lever the boat up, because it slid out when the boat capsized.

Your rudder should have first been secured as well. The sailor in Figure 1.23 had secured the rudder. He turned the boat around so that the sail

Figure 1.22. **(Photo courtesy of Dan Caplan Photography)**

Figure 1.23. (Photo courtesy of Dan Caplan Photography)

is downwind. When raising it, it will be coming up into the wind, which reduces the chance of it capsizing again.

The process of capsizing and righting the boat again can make you very wet and very tired quickly. Be cautious; dress so you will not get hypothermia. Wear clothing that does not absorb much water. It will help you stay dry and not get too heavy to climb aboard again. A paddle should be secured to the dinghy in case the wind or your skills as a sailor fail. A bucket should be tied on unless your boat is self-bailing, like a Sunfish or Laser. No boat with any kind of cabin, no matter how small, is entirely self-bailing. Any cabin boat should have a bilge pump, as well as a bucket and sponge.

Learn the wind

In most locations, the wind will frequently change direction and strength. It will be easier to sail once you learn to be aware of the wind.

DRILL. As you walk around, just going about your business, start to pay attention to the wind. You can feel it on your skin and on your hair. Notice it changes direction and strength as you move, because of your motion. If you are walking at three miles per hour, you create a wind you feel of that strength, which is added to the *actual wind*. The wind you feel on your skin is the *apparent wind*, the mix of the actual wind with the three-mile-per hour wind you create. As your boat moves, the wind will change direction and strength, too. You will adjust the sails to this, the apparent wind. This is easier than calculating the actual wind. Go with the force you feel.

"You can observe a lot just by watching."
YOGI BERRA

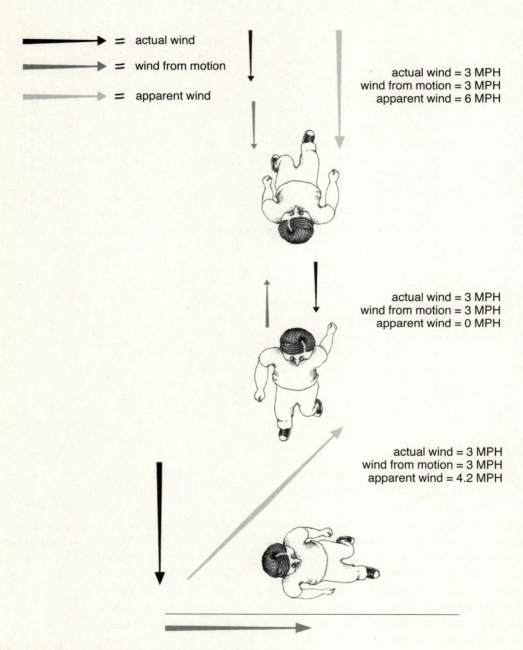

Figure 1-24. Apparent Wind. (Drawing by Clare Rosean)

You will find the wind changes direction, slows, or both when an obstruction blocks it. The wind will attempt to get around the obstruction. Even if the obstruction is downwind from you, the wind will still be deflected and slowed. Or, the obstruction can speed the wind passing nearby, forming what is called a wind tunnel. You may also find that in partly cloudy conditions, the wind gusts as each cloud or sunny spot goes past. A gust of even a few seconds can tip the boat. The solution is to let out the sails as necessary so they catch less wind, or hike out farther which will keep the boat reasonably upright.

THE SIXTH STEP: GO SAILING TODAY!

"When in doubt, let it out." All sail trim can be reduced to just that sentence. This fundamental concept will be repeated many times.

Trim the sails to start moving

Basic sail control is simple: let the sail out until it just starts to luff, then pull it in until it just fills. It is easier to sail if you determine the wind direction. Use the boat's wind indicator, look at flags, watch the clouds move, blow children's bubbles, or wet a finger and stick it into the breeze. Aim the boat at least 45 degrees from the wind direction. If you picture a clock with the wind coming toward the 12, you can sail no closer to the wind than pointing the boat in between the 10 and the 11, or the one and the two. Once you are aimed in any direction at least 45 degrees (an eighth of a circle) from the direction of the wind, all you have to do is let the sail out until it just starts to luff, then pull it back in until it just fills. What could be simpler? This is true regardless of the direction you

want to go. The sail's job, and your job controlling each sail, is to cause the wind to move quickly and smoothly along the curve of the sail. That moves the boat forward. In our step-by-step learning process, we'll talk more about this in Day Three and in detail in Appendix F. You do not need to know how electricity works to turn on a light. Nonetheless, there are times when understanding how sails work will enable you to improve your sailing technique.

Following are the steps for trimming the sails:

1. Use the correct sheet (the rope used to let the sail out and pull it in). Use it to let the sail out away from the *centerline* of the boat until the front of the sail no longer has a smooth, airplane wing–like shape. That is called luffing the sail. Then, pull it back in (with the same sheet) until the smooth shape is just restored.

2. If the sail is pulled as close to the centerline as it can go, and either the sail is not smooth or the boat is not moving well, turn the boat away from the wind until the sail is smooth and the boat is moving well. You may have to let the sail out a tiny bit, too.

3. If the boat is going downwind, let that same sheet out so the sail moves away from the centerline as far as it can go, or until it loses the wing-like shape (whichever happens first). Let it out on the side of the boat that is further from the direction the wind is coming from.

4. If the boat is tipping to the side more than you are comfortable with, let the sheet out until the boat levels a bit.

5. If the boat has more than one sail, do this with all the sails.

Figure 1.25.

Figure 1.26.

When you go sailing

What you should see: You should see some ripples in the water indicating a light wind. You should see yourself safely and comfortably on the deck or cockpit of the boat. You should look ahead and to both sides for other boats. You should visualize what the top surface of an airplane wing looks like from inside the wing. You should see most of the sail forming the smooth shape like the airplane wing. Do not worry if only half or so of the sail looks like that. You will learn over time how to fix that.

What you should not see: Clouds building vertically, especially forming an "anvil" top. Nor should you see a dark line of clouds moving toward you. Either means it is time to head for home—immediately.

What you should feel: The sheet connected to the bottom of the sail should pull in fairly easily until the sail starts to take the wing-like shape. Then, it will get much harder to pull in. You may feel the boat start to heel as it starts to move forward.

What you should hear: If the sail is out too far, it may make the noise of a flag whipping in the wind. You should hear only a little wind and water noise if the sails are set properly.

Remember always: The sail is set to about the same angle from the wind going past the boat. The sail will teach you the proper angle: After you let it out until it loses its wing-like shape (luffing), pull it in until the sail first takes its airplane wing–like shape. Regardless what direction the hull is pointed underneath the sail, the sail will fill properly when its angle to the wind you are feeling (the apparent wind) is correct.

Remember always: When in doubt, let it out. When the mast or other rigging, such as the wires holding up the mast, interferes, limiting how far the sail can be pulled in or let

It really is that simple. This works with each and every sail.

See an example of a luffing sail in Figure 1.25. The front of the sail has a series of waves in it; luffing usually looks like that. Luffing is the failure of the sail to take a smooth, airplane wing–like shape.

Compare the luffing sail with the overly trimmed sail in Figure 1.26.

The sail in Figure 1.26 looks good, but the sailor has failed to let it out until it luffs and then pull it in just until the luffing stops. The result: it's in too far and is stalled. The beginning sailor cannot tell the sail is over-trimmed just by looking at it. Both luffing and over-trimming slow the boat. Thus, the rule to follow to keep the sail adjusted correctly is: "When in doubt, let it out." Then pull it back in until the sail just fills; it gets its wing-like shape. Learn over time to let it out ever so slightly, until you get the first hint the sail is luffing, and then pull it in just to the point luffing stops.

out, that may keep you from adjusting the sail to its most efficient point. That's okay.

The wind will force the sail to be on one side of the boat. That might not let you travel in the direction you desire. This may require tacking or jibing. We will learn tacking today and save jibing for another day. You may see a reference to the "circle of sailing" in other books. Ignore that. Set the sail for the wind you feel. It is true no boat powered by sails can go directly, or nearly directly, into the wind, but other than that truth, the "circle of sailing" is just a confusing complication for the beginner to overcome.

In Figure 1.27, you can see that, regardless of the direction of the boat, the sail will best fill at a constant angle to the apparent wind.

Figure 1.27.
(Drawing by
Clare Rosean)

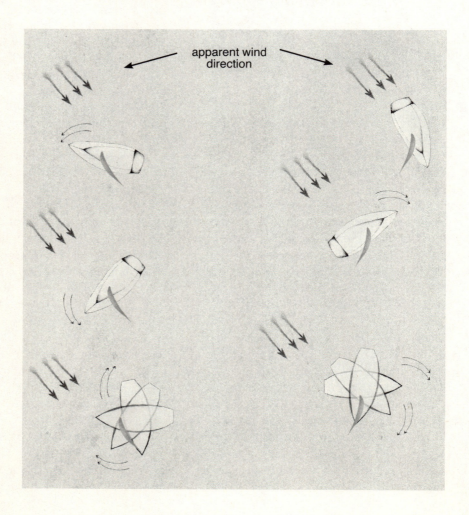

If the boat stops

Look at the sails. Are they full or not?

1. Sails not full. Possible causes:
   a. No or very little wind. Solutions:
      1.) Check for any slight wind. Blow bubbles. See which way they go.
      2.) Look for smoke, waves, or other clues to see if you are misreading the wind.
      3.) Wait a while. If nothing changes, row or start the engine.
   b. There is wind, but you may be heading too directly into the wind, which is the "cannot sail" zone. Solutions:
      1.) Look up at the wind indicators, or blow bubbles. If they indicate the wind is straight ahead, or nearly so, you must turn the boat at least a bit away from the wind until the sails can fill. If you cannot turn because you are not moving, let the wind back the boat up until you can turn while going backwards, then adjust the sails, and you will automatically be able to go forward again.
      2.) Make the boat tilt (heel) away from the wind. Most of the time we sailors are trying to make the boat tilt less. But a little bit of tilt away from the wind helps the sails fill, because gravity is pulling on the sails in the same direction the wind is trying to fill them. Also, a little bit of tilt may mean less friction of the boat's hull in the water. Most sailboats are designed to sail faster with some heeling.
2. Sails are full. Possible causes:
   a. You have pulled the sails in too tight, so they are stalled and ineffective. Solution: Adjust them in the usual manner—let them out a bit until they lose shape, then pull them back in until they just form the wing-like shape.
   b. You have run aground. Solution: tilt the boat or raise the centerboard.

"HEAD UP!" "HEAD DOWN!"
"UPWIND!" "DOWNWIND!"

These terms are especially confusing to the beginner. *Head up* means turn upwind, more toward the wind, and *head down* means turn downwind, turning away from the wind. But which way is that? Where is the wind coming from? Until you know, just look at the sails. The sails are on one side or the other. To sail more downwind, point the boat more to the side the sails are on. To "head up" point the boat more to the side the sails are not on.

How much is enough? Usually, if you are told to head up, turn gently until the sails just start to luff (see Figure 1.25) then turn back very slightly until the sails fill. If you are told to head down, turn away from the wind, that is turn the boat toward the side the sails are sitting on, until the sails fill again. If the command is repeated immediately, picture a clock face, and try turning the boat as far along a clock circle as a minute hand would move in three minutes or until you are told to stop turning, whichever happens first.

It is okay to ask how far to turn.

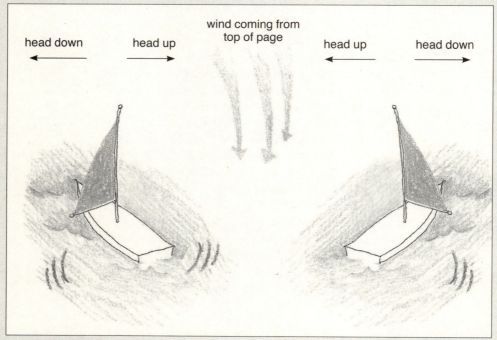

(Drawing by Clare Rosean)

Basic steering

You will steer today!

1. The boat may turn differently than a car or bicycle. This is because the rudder is in the rear. It is in water, which has less grip than a tire on land, so its effect is not instantaneous. The slower you are going, the less grip and less response the rudder has. In slow going or big waves, the rudder will have to be turned more than at speed in flat water.
2. The turn begins as the rear of the boat swings out in response to the rudder. If the boat has a tiller, which is a stick attached to the rudder instead of a steering wheel as in a car, the stick is turned left to turn the boat right, and vice versa.
3. Changes in wind, waves, and boat speed will affect the boat's direction. Over time, you will learn to make subtle steering adjustments often, perhaps constantly.
4. You will have to be aware of your surroundings. Unlike driving, when almost everyone is travelling nearly the same speed and following the road, boat speeds differ by a lot. Boats and obstructions can come from any direction. Keep looking around.
5. Before you leave the dock, survey your sailing territory. Review it by eye, and consult the relevant chart. Bridges, obstructions, and shallows or submerged rocks are usually well charted but not always marked on the water. Learn where any near you are located. Things under and above the surface can be a problem. Your mast may not clear a bridge or a wire. Wires in particular can be very dangerous, often carrying many thousands of volts, way more than household power.
6. Learn and follow the "Rules of the Road." A very basic version follows.
7. If you cannot adjust the sails while holding onto the tiller or wheel, you cannot sail that boat today without at least one crew.

When you are actually steering

What you should see: You should be able to see ahead and in all directions away from the boat. This may mean you will have to move around, because the sails may be preventing you from seeing past them. You may need to move to the side or bend down to look underneath the sail at least every few minutes, more frequently if the area is crowded. You should see some wind indicator telling you the direction and possibly the speed of the wind.

What you should feel: You should feel a little pressure on the tiller or wheel. The pressure should try to turn the boat a bit toward the wind. You should feel the wind on your face and body and be able to determine its direction. The wind you feel should agree generally with the wind indicator and will vary throughout the day in direction and strength. You will feel the boat rock up and down, side to side, and be pushed a bit from the course you choose.

When steering, you have more ways to deal with a strong wind. We've mentioned letting the sails out if the boat is tilting too much or making it hard to steer. When steering, you can turn slightly into the wind so that the wind pressure on the sails is reduced, but you still have enough speed to steer. Or head away from the wind (this is called *bearing off*) to reduce the side pressure on the sails.

Remember always: When going away from the wind, never let the wind reach the danger zone where it can catch the sail from the other side without being prepared to do a maneuver called a *jibe*. In a jibe, with the wind at the boat's stern the boat is turned so that the sail switches to the other side. This can cause the sail's motion to be sudden and even violent if not controlled. You'll learn the jibe maneuver soon, but not today. Do not risk an accidental jibe. See Figure 1.28.

Remember, the wind can shift direction at any time. The rougher the water, and the shiftier the wind, the further you must steer the boat from the danger zone.

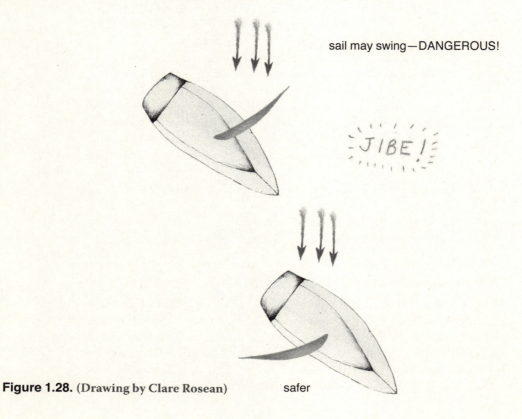

sail may swing—DANGEROUS!

JIBE!

safer

Figure 1.28. (Drawing by Clare Rosean)

Rules of the road

Rule number one is: avoid everyone and everything. Suppose there is another boat, swimmer, or obstruction nearby. What should you do? At this stage you are like the person who has just learned to ride a bicycle. You do not know the rules regarding who has the right-of-way. So, just avoid everything. You can shout questions to the other vessels, but Rule No. 1 is turn to avoid anything and everything. Turn sharply so others know your intentions.

Learn the right-of-way rules for the purpose of giving way to the privileged boat and not to seek to enforce your rights whenever you can. While covered by no rule, do not try to bull your way to the harbor entrance first. The other boat may have some emergency. The complete Rules of the Road are found in the U.S. Coast Guard publication of that name. This book has a simpler and conservative version. Courtesy and Rule No. 1 (avoid anything and everything) will give you the margin of safety you need. When passing (if you must!), give as much room as you can. Avoid those who do not know the rules by using Right-of-Way Rule No. 1: Stay out of the way of everyone and everything. However, there is an advantage of predictability. If you have right-of-way, and the other vessel is aware of its responsibility, you do not want to confuse the other skipper by making unpredictable avoidance maneuvers. That is the reason to switch from Rule No. 1 to the rest of the rules.

It is always best to plan to pass behind another boat instead of attempting to cross in front. The exception is only if you are certain you will easily cross in front.

When you are under sail, you have right-of-way over all small- to medium-size powerboats. For ships, observe the "rule of tonnage": Stay out of the way of all large ships. They simply cannot maneuver around you without miles of advance warning. Their speed can be deceptive. Especially if the ship is just leaving the harbor area, it may be subtly but substantially increasing speed. Aided by AIS (a read-out of the ship's name and time and location of its closest approach), a call notifying that ship by name of your presence and asking if they see you is appropriate, but do not attempt to get in their way. While the Rule of Tonnage is not a formal rule, it is a life saver and should be violated no more often than the law of gravity.

Remember, you can tell if you are on a collision course by watching the background behind the other vessel. If the vessel is moving forward against the background, it will pass in front. If moving backward against the background, it will pass behind. If it is not moving against the background, you are on a collision course. You can avoid collision by altering course or by changing speed.

After Rule No. 1 and the Rule of Tonnage comes the rule that **actually, *no boat ever has complete right-of-way*.** While a casual reading of the rules may make one think one boat may have right-of-way over another, and the phrase is often used, this is an oversimplification at best. You never have right-of-way. You are, with respect to powerboats, the *stand-on* vessel, and the powerboat must give way. But, in the event of a collision, both vessels and both captains can be held at fault.

There are 37 rules under the International Regulations for Preventing Collisions at Sea (COLREGS), which apply in international waters as marked on your charts. These are similar to the U.S. rules, which apply in the Great Lakes, coastal areas, and inland waterways.

With that in mind, the COLREGS and American rules generally give stand-on rights to the less maneuverable, and *give-way* requirements to the more maneuverable. Note that if your engine is running, even with your sails up, under the rules you are a powerboat.

As a sailboat, the COLREGS and American rules are consistent with Rule No. 1. You give way to all vessels that cannot maneuver or have difficulty maneuvering. This includes anchored vessels, vessels not under command (such as a ship that has lost power or steering; treat any ship not moving as not under command), vessels that are engaged in commercial fishing, and (under the COLREGS only) vessels that must stay in a narrow channel because of their *draft*. To that group add those under the Rule of Tonnage, although that is not a COLREG.

As a sailboat, you not only give way to unpowered (rowing) craft, you stay far enough away that your wake does not disturb them.

When passing any vessel, you give way to them. Even a sailboat passing a powerboat gives way to the powerboat.

When under power or using both power and sails ("powersailing" or "motorsailing"), you give way to sailboats, and boats you are crossing from their left. "When you are on the right, you are in the right" is a good way to remember this rule—except you never actually have "right-of-way."

Stand-on and give-way rules between sailboats require you to understand the phrases *starboard tack* and *port tack*, as well as upwind and *downwind*.

It will help you remember if you place a little letter P on the left side of the boom, and a little letter S on the right side of the boom, obviously standing for port and starboard. If the letter P is visible on the boom from the cockpit, and the wind is coming over the left/port side of the boat, you are on port tack. The confusing aspect is that on port tack, the boom and sail are to the starboard side of the boat. The letter P on the boom will remind you. Conversely, with the S visible, wind from the right, but the boom off to the port side, you are on starboard tack.

Applying this, if you are on port tack you give way to vessels on starboard tack and to those whose tack you cannot ascertain. The starboard-tack vessel is the stand-on vessel. If on the same tack, the windward vessel gives way. This can be a problem for the give-way vessel operating under spinnaker, but that is the rule in the books. Be courteous, and use Rule No. 1 for boats under spinnaker.

Under the racing rules, a vessel approaching a shallow or obstruction, even if it is the windward or port-tack vessel, may have to be given right-of-way. This rule should be applied as a courtesy outside of the race course.

Racing vessels do not have right-of-way over cruisers. As a courtesy, give them the ability to stand on, preferably without positioning your boat directly upwind and nearby them, partially blocking their wind, *blanketing* them. Stay seven mast lengths away. While your starboard-tack vessel has right-of-way over a racer on port, consider that you may ruin their day, or their season championship, enforcing your rights. Is that worth shaving 30 seconds off a pleasant voyage?

In Figure 1.29, your boat, *Helen* in the drawing, is headed toward *Betty*, *Alice*, and *Cathy*. If your boat is gaining on *Betty*, you must pass either to windward or leeward. It is better manners, but slower, to pass to leeward. You will interfere less with *Betty*'s wind. If *Betty*

is heading upwind as best she can, you may struggle to head more upwind than her. *Alice* and *Cathy* may alter course a bit to avoid each other. Do you need to avoid *Alice* and *Cathy*? Look at the background beyond each. If *Alice* or *Cathy* is moving forward against the background, she will pass ahead. If *Alice* or *Cathy* is moving backward against the background, you will pass ahead. Be sure when attempting to pass ahead that you have plenty of clearance.

Where is it safe to sail? First, look at your *chart*. Then, watch where the other sailboats are going. Even more importantly, watch where other sailboats do *not* go. If only small sailboats

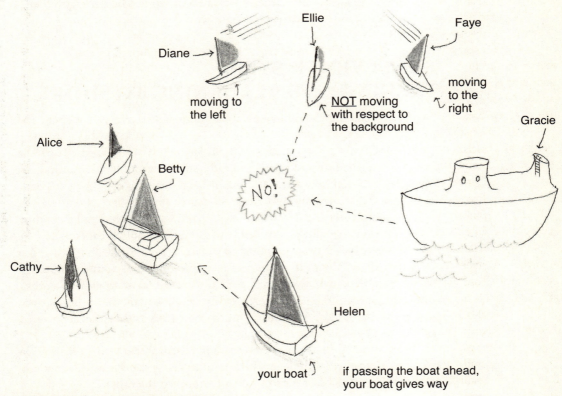

Figure 1.29. (Drawing by Clare Rosean)

go to a particular area, determine if your boat has too much draft to safely go there. Look at the chart, your map of the harbor area. (Have the most detailed map available, a large-scale map of a small area.) Can you see why it is safe to go where the boats are going? Can you see why they aren't going to particular places? Ask someone, or go to the navigation section of this book, Day Six.

Simplified rules of steering

1. The boat may turn the opposite way you expect. Be ready for that.
2. The boat will not track as straight as a car. It can gently "slide," usually in the direction the wind, current, and waves want to take it.
3. You can control your direction only if your boat is moving through the water.
4. Under sail, you cannot steer directly into the wind.
5. Avoid any and all obstacles. Learn the Rules of the Road. Watch out for swimmers. Other boats are best avoided by aiming to their sterns and letting them pass ahead.

THE SEVENTH STEP: TACKING AND RETURNING TO SHORE

Two basic maneuvers combining sail handling and steering are tacking and jibing.

We will learn tacking today. Without tacking, we cannot safely turn the boat even one-half turn today. We could not return to the beach or harbor. We have discussed how sailboats cannot head straight into the wind. Sailboats must travel no closer than about 45 degrees to port or starboard (left or right) of the actual wind direction. The zone directly upwind and extending 45 degrees on either side is impossible to sail in and is often called the *no-go zone*. When we want to sail our boat to a place in the no-go zone, we cannot go directly there. We must go to port or starboard of the destination, much like we must remain on the road in a car and cannot travel straight to a destination through buildings. Instead, we drive along a road, off to the south or perhaps to the right of our house, and then turn left at the intersection that takes us to an avenue straight home.

We do something similar when sailing. The water isn't the obstruction that equates to the buildings; it is the wind. We zigzag our way against the wind, first on one side of the no-go zone, and then the other.

HANDLING THE SHEETS

As crew, you may be asked to tack or handle the sheets. "Sheet out" means ease the sheet out. It is okay to ask for a lot or a little, but if "sheet out" is screamed, release the sheet until the sail is luffing. "Sheet in" means to pull the rope in, which brings the sail closer into the boat. When you sheet out, you may have to remove the sheet from a cleat or other mechanism, and if it is around a winch, you may have to remove several turns of the rope from around the winch.

Caution: Assume the rope is under tension and be careful. Leave one wrap around the winch to assist you in controlling its release.

When we go from one side of the no-go zone to the other, we turn through a quarter of a circle. During that turn, the sails are unable to work. The sails move across the boat from one side to the other as the boat turns. The boat has turned enough when we can set the sails in a wing-like shape on the other side.

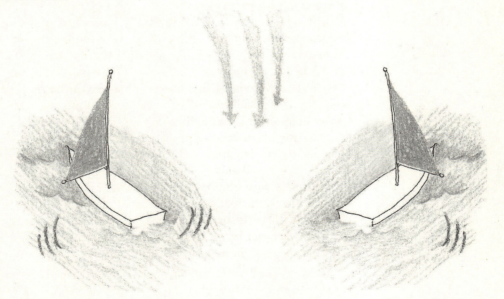

Figure 1.30. Tacking equals changing direction—so the bow goes through the wind and the sail switches sides. The boat heels accordingly. (Drawing by Clare Rosean)

Since the sails are luffing and ineffective during the tack, only the momentum of the boat will enable you to complete the tack successfully. The wind is blowing against the boat, slowing it down. A tack must be done smartly, quickly, and efficiently so you don't lose all the momentum and come to a halt. If you do get stopped, use the twelfth step below.

During a tack you will feel the wind coming around the bow of the boat. It will start on one side, go past the bow, and end up on the other side. You will feel the sheets go slack and then tension up as you finish the tack with the wind on the other side.

You will see the jib sheets go slack, although the mainsheet sometimes does not slacken. You will see the sails luff as you continue the turn, only to be filled on the other side of the boat.

You will release the jib sheet on one side and tension it on the other side.

You may hear more noise as winches are ground and the sails noisily luff. This is nothing to be concerned about and is perfectly normal.

The steps to a good tack

The short version is: you will be making a turn of a quarter of a circle, through the no-go zone. As a crew member you will be handling a jib:

1. When the captain says prepare to tack, get ready to release the jib sheet that is under tension.
2. When the captain asks "ready to tack?", answer "ready" as soon as you can be ready.
3. When the captain says "coming about" or "hard to lee," that means he has begun the tack.
4. When the sail begins to luff, release the sheet that was under tension.
5. Sheet in on the other side. Take up the slack, and tension the sheet on the new side. It is easier to sheet in before the wind starts to fill the sail.

Congratulations. A perfect tack.

Here are the details as captain:

1. Identify the wind direction.
2. Have the sail control lines ready.
3. Visualize the sail on the other side of the boat, shaped and pulled in properly.
4. Look around. Be sure you will not get in the way of other boats or head to an obstacle.

5. If you have crew aboard, call out "ready to tack?" Have the crew answer "ready." This is so crew will be prepared for the maneuver.

6. Skipper and crew must be prepared to move to the opposite side of the boat and be ready with the sheets.

7. Before the tack, aim the boat about an eighth of a turn from the wind; in other words, aim at about a 45- to 50-degree angle from the wind. Do not worry about measuring that. Just have the sails full and moving the boat well and have the wind seem to come from somewhat ahead. (As you gain experience, you will be able to sail with the bow pointed closer to the wind direction.)

8. When you (and your crew) are ready, call "helm's a lee" and push the tiller or turn the wheel as far as you can. You want to move the front of the boat through a bit more than a quarter turn. At the midpoint of the turn the bow will head briefly directly into the wind. Through most of this turn, the boat will be slowed by wind. It is important to turn quickly enough that the boat does not stop and can complete the turn. At the end the wind will be coming over the other side of the bow, and the sail will be filled by the wind on the other side of the boat. So if before the tack the wind is to the left, turn the boat sharply to the left. If the wind is to the right, turn right. As you gain experience, you may make your turn more subtle and work toward turning through the minimum change in direction necessary.

9. While the boat is turning, release the sheet that is holding the jib sail close to the boat. Let the sail go across the boat to the other side. If it gets caught on something, turn back to your earlier heading and figure out what it got caught on. If you conclude the sail just needed a little help to get it around, try again giving the sail that help. The main sail should need little or no adjustment when tacking. It should just go to the other side on its own; be wary of the boom.

10. Once the boat is more than midway through the turn, and the sail is even slightly on the other side, use the sheet from the new side to pull the jib sail in.

11. Let the sails fill on the new tack. Build up a little speed and bring the boat's angle closer to the wind but not so close as to lose headway. Over time, work toward finding the best angle for speed upwind and maintaining that speed and angle. You will learn more about this in Day Three. As the wind changes in speed and direction, steer to compensate.

12. If you should have the boat stop during the tack, and it is facing the wind, just let the wind back up the boat. You can continue to turn

while backing up. To help you turn if you are stuck facing the wind, you can push the mainsail out into the wind.

After tacking, if you want to turn further from the wind, do so, and adjust the sails. Keep practicing. Keep sailing.

Congratulations. A great tack.

As you sail

Stay close to shore and the beach or harbor. Head a little upwind. Bring in the sail when it starts to luff, and let it out until it fills. Make slight turns, continuing to let out and pull in the sail as described. Make a mental note of the changes in wind speed, wind direction, boat speed, and boat direction. Note also the angle of heel and how it increases as you head upwind and decreases downwind.

Notice that the mainsheet, except in the smallest dinghies, has many parts. That is for leverage. The traveler is connected to the mainsheet. For today, just leave the traveler in the center.

Once you are comfortable, you can raise the jib if you wish. As you raise it be sure you will not drift into other boats or obstructions. The jib gets adjusted with the jib sheet to the same wing-like shape as the main.

You are sailing! Continue changing direction and adjusting the sails accordingly. A reminder: Be sure not to risk a jibe. Keep the boat pointed so that the wind is not coming from a direction, i.e., behind, that threatens a jibe with a wind shift.

Has the wind changed direction or speed? Where is the wind coming from? How can you tell where the wind is coming from? You have wind indicators, but you also have your skin, the sails, bits of cloth on and near the sails, other boats, flags, clouds, and smoke to show the wind direction, which will vary a bit. Always be aware of obstacles and the wind direction. Continue to ease and pull in the sails as you would to adjust for a change in the wind direction. Turn the boat a slight amount toward the wind. Adjust the sails to compensate. What did that do to the sails? You should have brought the sail in closer to the boat. Next, turn the boat a bit away from the wind, and adjust the sails to compensate. Move around a little bit to see how your position on the boat affects it and to make certain you are seeing any objects or other boats in all directions.

DRILL. Now, if you have room to do so safely, turn the boat gradually into the wind and pull the sails gradually in as well. Try to get the boat to sail in a direction about 45 degrees from the actual wind. This may be 30 degrees from the apparent wind. Concentrate on upwind sailing; the other angles from the wind are easier. The wind will be shifting in direction and speed. Adjust your heading and sails. Try tacking, using the techniques previously described.

A reminder: On your first sail, stay within a 15-minute sail of the harbor. Do not go too far from help, and certainly not out of sight of land, but sail until you get used to the feeling of the boat, the steering, and the effect of the ever-changing wind on the sails. If the wind speed drops, you will feel the boat heel less, the wind will seem to come even more from straight ahead, and the sails may flap uselessly. If the wind entirely goes away, you may want to motor a while. If you get tired or cold, or the weather changes and looks like it might get worse, it is time to head in.

Returning to the beach

As you approach the beach, be aware of the depth of the water. Depending on the clarity of the water, you may be able to estimate the depth you are in just by looking. Other depth indicators are people standing in the water, breaking waves (waves tend to break at a depth one half the wave height), boats and other objects in the water, and the distance from the beach.

Slow down as you approach, and start to raise the rudder and centerboard or daggerboard in small steps. You do not want the centerboard or rudder to hit bottom, especially at higher speeds. Raising the centerboard and rudder makes controlling the direction of the boat a little more difficult. The steering effectiveness is reduced, and the directional stability is reduced as well.

Watch out for swimmers, especially near beaches and shorelines.

Continue to sail in to the beach, and continue to lift the centerboard/daggerboard and rudder as necessary to keep them from touching the bottom. You can sail in all the way until the boat hits the bottom or step out in knee-deep water and guide the boat in.

Do not allow the sail to be blown around when you are not sailing. This puts unnecessary wear on the sail. Consider it the same as revving your car engine while parked. Shut off your engine; tie the sail down. Do not allow sails to be exposed to the sun unnecessarily.

Returning to the dock

Imagine you are driving to a parking space. But instead of using the brakes, you approach with the transmission in neutral and drift along to a halt. Now, add the effect of current and wind.

Yet, you want to just touch the parking space at the point you become almost motionless.

This is similar to the challenge of docking a sailboat. Yet it is not as difficult as it sounds. Full speed in open water in a sailboat is maybe eight miles per hour. Docking (parking) speed is maybe 1/8 of that, or one mile per hour, 1½ feet per second. Your sailboat is slowed to whatever speed you choose by letting the sails luff more than fill. At that speed, your greatest dangers are (1) boredom, and (2) embarrassment. While you do not have brakes, you could let the sails luff or push them out so the wind hits them in a direction to slow the boat. However, you cannot slow the boat by luffing sails if you are travelling downwind.

PROCEDURE AND DRILL. Do a few dry runs. Have dock lines and fenders ready, attached to the boat. Pick a spot with similar conditions of wind and current. You can judge the direction and strength of the current at any point by seeing its effect upon buoys or posts in the water. Look at the waves made by the current on buoys or posts. There is no need, and it is inappropriate, to throw objects in the water just to measure current. The object may be driven more by the wind than the current. Make a pretend approach, using an imaginary dock. If you turn into the wind, or the current, the wind or current will help you by slowing you to a stop and even may send you backwards. Try it. If you approach a dock with the wind or current behind you, it will speed you up, so this is not to be done by the beginner. You can slow yourself with opposing wind or current, your rudder swung all the way to one side and then the other (keeping you generally going straight), fenders, and, finally, the crush space of the hull (which you should know is generally non-existent). Conversely, some boats can be *sculled* forward with rapid swings of the rudder. After you've done a pretend approach or two and feel ready, approach the actual dock. Remember your steering, the wind, and the current. If there are three crew aboard, have one in front, one in the middle, and one at the stern, each ready with lines. If sailing in, be ready to drop the sails to stop the boat as soon as it is tied. To throw a line to someone on the dock, be sure it is not tangled; if so, it will fall short. Coil the line in one direction. When throwing the line, flick your wrist in the opposite direction so the line tends to uncoil as it is thrown.

Remember, the slower your speed through the water, the less turning effect your rudder has. Comparatively strong steering motions may be required. When you get close enough, get a line quickly wrapped onto a cleat on the dock, and quickly do the same on the other end of the boat, so both bow and stern are secured. Usually, you will attach a stern line first, because you are nearest the stern while steering. Also, if the boat is moving forward, the stern line will hold the boat in to the dock.

This means your approach should be planned to get the stern of the boat closest to the dock. The boat could spin around and away from the dock when the boat is attached at one end only. This is especially true if your crew attaches a bow line only as you head to the dock. You could also have lines rigged at the dock that you left behind when you headed out; this is convenient and recommended. You could then just reach out, grab the lines, and set them onto the cleats or winches of the boat. If you are going slowly, these lines will easily stop the boat without harm—just keep your fingers clear.

If the lines are on the boat, it is necessary to step off the boat to tie the lines to the pier. Step, not jump. It is dangerous to jump off a boat. The skipper must maneuver close enough to the dock so that he and/or the crew can step to the pier, with mooring line in hand and enough slack on the mooring line that no one will be pulled off the pier. Quickly wrap the lines around nearby cleats.

If approaching a mooring, try to come to a stop right at it, in reach of it, using much the same

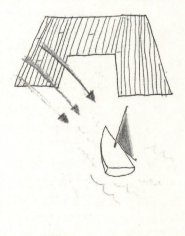

Figure 1.31. Consider the wind and the current. (Drawing by Clare Rosean)

techniques as you would approaching a dock. Your advantage in approaching a mooring is that you can approach upwind regardless of the wind direction, controlling the power of the sails (pulled in to power up or allowed to luff to slow down), and slowing as you approach to maintain a safe speed.

Tie up completely. See the drawing in Figure 1.32 for an example of a boat tied to a dock to one side. Notice there are two lines each to the bow and the stern. The two longer lines, called *spring lines*, resist the boat's motion forward and back. Once the boat is secured, see how other boats are tied, and get advice on dealing with any currents or tides at the mooring.

Whether at anchor or in a mooring, any line can fray or chafe. For general mooring use in protected areas a wrapping of anti-chafe tape is advisable. For long-term use, or in storms, lengths of thick cloth or, better, leather should be wrapped around any parts of lines that can rub against another or the boat. Rubbing or stretching lines can overheat them from friction, weakening them and causing them to part. Thus, some air or water

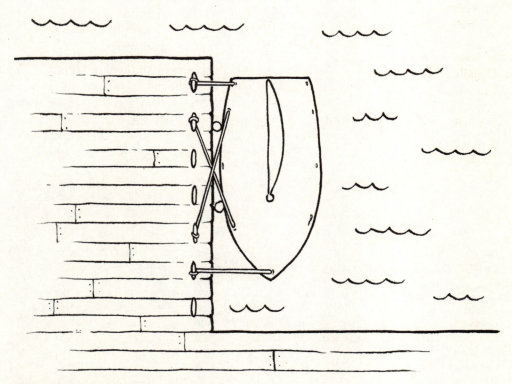

Figure 1.32. (Drawing by Christopher Hoyt)

Figure 1.33. Chafe points.
(Drawing by Clare Rosean)

flow is desirable inside chafe coverings. Crossing lines is to be avoided unless chafe protection is thorough (see Figure 1.33).

Just before you leave, lift the outboard engine out of the water. It is left in the water until you leave so the coolant will not drain out while the engine is still hot.

Fold the sails and stow the gear

If the sails are dry, fold them and place them in their bag. The mainsail is usually folded onto the boom. If the mast has to be lowered, as in a boat being trailered, try rolling the mainsail onto the boom and stowing the boom and mainsail together.

If wet, spread the sails out to dry. Do not fold wet sails. "Ridden hard and put away wet" is a recipe for shortening sail life.

Figure 1.34 (left). This sail is dry and being folded properly. I usually start at the bottom of the sail and lay folds of a convenient size on the bottom section.

Figure 1.35 (right). Denise is happy the sail is folded. Now it can be rolled up from her end and placed in the sail bag.

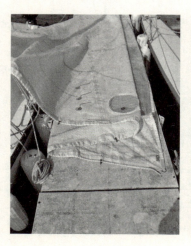

Put the boat cushions on edge so they do not trap any water underneath. Lock up.

Enjoy your dinner, and share your stories with your friends. Tell them that you and your book are going sailing again the next nice day and that you will learn to jibe. You have completed the seven manageable, small, fun projects to become a sailor. Over the next six days, you will learn additional skills.

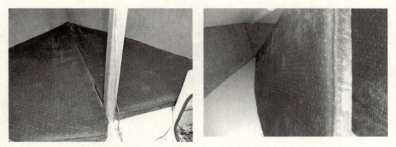

Figure 1.36 (left) and 1.37 (right). Stored on edge, only a small portion of the cushion is in contact with the fiberglass. Even if the fiberglass is dry when you leave, condensation or leaks can play havoc with the cushions if they are not set on edge.

IMPROVE YOUR SKILLS:

The Jibe, Steering, Boating Etiquette

> *"What can we gain by sailing to the moon if we are not able to cross the abyss that separates us from ourselves? This is the most important of all voyages . . ."*
>
> THOMAS MERTON

THE EIGHTH STEP: THE JIBE

What we will learn:

With the jibe, our last basic maneuver, we can steer our boat in all directions possible to sail in. We will continue to learn to sail a little better in each direction.

A jibe differs from a tack because, in a jibe, the boat is turned so that the wind passes directly behind the boat, not in front as in a tack. At some point in the jibe, the mainsail will suddenly feel the full force of the wind behind, snapping it across. This is why we talked about a danger zone in Day One. It is often better to circle around nearly a full turn to tack than to turn only slightly and jibe. This is especially true for the novice, or in stronger winds.

The boom, and the mainsail attached to it, is controlled by its line (the mainsheet). Sheet the main in as much as possible before jibing, so the boom will have less room to swing freely across. (However, some boats, such as the Laser, will not tolerate this.) Once the boom swings across, the main should be promptly let out as much as needed. The crew's function in jibing is the same as in tacking, except the crew must be even more wary of the boom.

You must control the jibe. The boom may move without warning in a poorly controlled or accidental jibe. Time the jibe so that it occurs in relatively light wind, or while going particularly fast, such as surfing down a wave, either or both of which reduce the amount of force of the wind.

So, the procedure for jibing is:

1. Locate the wind direction.
2. Locate the direction you want to head the boat in, and be sure your new heading will not conflict with other boats or obstructions.
3. Visualize the entire procedure: how the boat is to be turned; how the sails are to be adjusted.
4. Wait until the wind is momentarily relatively light.
5. Call out "ready to jibe?" if you have others aboard. Ask them to confirm they are ready.
6. Remember that the boat will heel to the opposite direction as before and may do so suddenly so those below decks should be advised with your call as well as those on deck.
7. Call out "jibe ho!"
8. Sheet in the mainsheet so it is nearer the centerline, and begin your turn to the direction you want the boat to head.
9. If necessary, help the mainsail across to the other side. Grab the mainsheet, and, otherwise staying clear of it and the boom, help it swing to the other side. If you hold the mainsheet between the sail and the fitting on the boat, hold it with your hand positioned so you can let go of the lines as they swing over. Some smaller boats allow you to control the jibe that way. Do not attempt to control the mainsheet as it swings from one side to the other until you have observed its movement, are certain you have the arm and hand strength to control it, and can keep the rest of your body safely clear of the sheet and the boom.
10. Adjust the mainsail for the new heading, if necessary.
11. Bring the jib to the other side, if desired.
12. Keep out of the wind danger zone. Refer to Figure 1.28. Keep the mainsail so it is pointed as far from the wind as possible. Look above at the wind indicator and behind you to try to pick out wind shifts. Waves and wind gusts may turn the boat and have the potential to cause an unintended jibe. So, larger waves and gusty or shifty winds make a larger danger zone.

13. Many sailors rig a preventer, a line tied to the boom and then forward to the hull on the side the boom is on, so that the boom can barely move.

Now, you can sail in all directions a sailboat can travel in.

Let's review downwind sailing. Upwind and downwind are relative terms. For this day's purposes, we can say we are sailing downwind any time the mainsail cannot go far enough away from the centerline of the boat to keep the smooth airflow on the outside of the sail. Upwind, the objective is to get the air flowing smoothly across the sails. Downwind, we cannot always do this. The ability to let the sail out is limited by the wires holding up the mast and the length of the mainsheet, whichever is more restricting.

When sailing downwind, the sails may look right, but the flow around the sail is not smooth. That is okay, because we do not need the maximum efficiency from the sails. Since we are probably not fighting the waves, which usually travel in the direction of the wind, and the resistance from the air friction on the hull and structures of the boat does not slow us, maximum efficiency isn't as important. Since the wind is from behind, friction from the sails and boat parts actually helps the boat move. For downwind sailing, the issue is to keep the boat under control while using sufficient sail area. Usually, the boat is tilting much less downwind than upwind, because the sails push the boat more forward than to the side. With the waves generally going the same direction as the boat, the hull isn't pounding through the waves, and the ride is more comfortable.

In the absence of large waves, sailing downwind is the easiest direction to sail. There is little more to do than raise the sails, let them out away from the centerline as much as possible while having them fill with air, watch ahead and around for boats and obstructions, verify that your course and weather are safe, relax, and enjoy.

THE NINTH STEP: IMPROVE YOUR STEERING

In some ways, the rudder is like a brake. Moving it a little will slow the boat a little. Moving it a lot will slow the boat a lot. Any time you turn the rudder, more of it will be dragging against the water.

EXPERIMENT. Compare pulling a knife blade through a sink full of water straight on versus dragging it at an angle to the direction of travel. You can see how a rudder at an unnecessary angle will slow the boat.

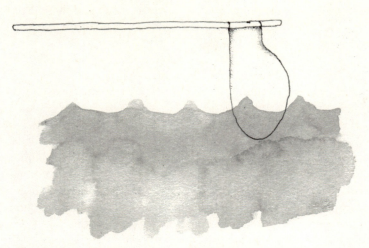

Figure 2.1. Turn the tiller as little as possible to keep on course. (Drawing by Clare Rosean)

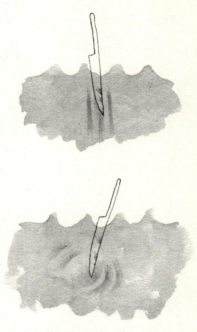

Figure 2.2. The rudder at an angle slows the boat. Compare the drag of a knife through water at different angles. (Drawing by Clare Rosean)

Proper seamanship calls for subtle adjustments to keep the boat on course; a gentle and persistent hand is best.

Notice, too, that a number of things can cause the boat to change its heading and call for a compensating touch on the rudder. As the boat's angle of heel changes, the boat will want to turn. Changes in the amount or direction of wind can require turning the rudder. Waves will try to push the boat off course. Even people moving about the boat will affect it. Pick an object in the distance, and keep your course with respect to it, moving the rudder with as subtle a touch as will suffice to generally point the boat in the correct direction.

If you watch carefully, you will see the boat is travelling in a slightly different direction than it is pointed in. Cars and bikes do not usually do that. Their tires have a better grip on the road than your boat does in the water. The boat's keel provides its grip. But, like a knife in the water, pushing it can make it move to the side. On a moving boat, the sideways push is always there from wind and waves. So you need a good keel. With a good keel, your boat will move much more in the correct direction than with a keel that is too shallow or poorly designed. The faster you go, the better the keel will work. It takes speed to sail upwind.

Figure 2.3. Note the tiller is set for a slight upwind turn. (Drawing by Clare Rosean)

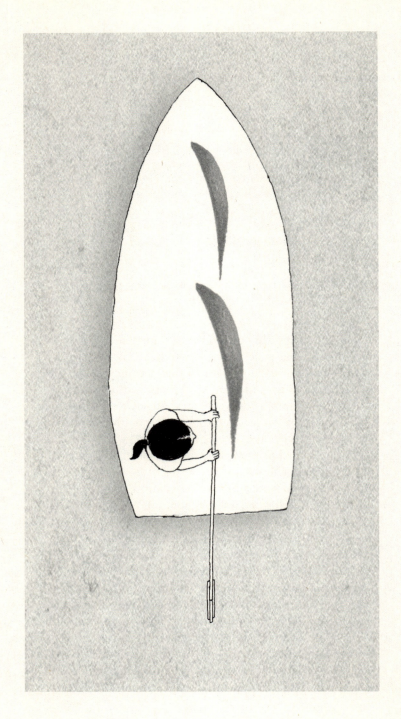

Upwind steering

Let us try to sail closer to the wind's direction than before. This will be a long-term learning process. Each boat you sail will be a bit different, but the principles are the same.

We haven't yet learned much about sail trim and subtle sail adjustment. What we will learn today, and continue in the future, is to get more out of our boat by combining some subtle changes in steering with some basic sail trim.

Sailing upwind well will be a joy if the weather isn't extreme. The breeze will be strongest heading upwind, because our boat speed is adding to the wind's speed. The boat will heel over a bit. In reasonable amounts, this can be both safe and thrilling.

For sailing upwind to the maximum, don't adjust the sails in the usual manner, that is, don't let them out until they just luff, then pull them in until they just fill. Instead, pull on the sheets to pull the sails in, almost but not quite all the way. Try leaving them out just an inch or two from the maximum inward position. This will give the sails a little more power than if they were in their maximum inward position. Steer to keep the sails in proper trim.

Let us pretend we cannot pull the sails in any more, nor do we want to let them out. So, how will we let the sails out until they luff and pull them in until they just fill? We will turn the entire boat, so that the sails just fill. This will involve a slight turn away from the wind. Once the sails fill, we will ever so slightly, slowly, turn in the direction of the wind and keep gently turning into the wind until the sails ever so slightly start to luff. That way, we know we are heading as close into the wind as possible. As soon as the sails slightly luff, the boat speed will decrease. Turn very slightly so the sails fill again. Note the speed of the boat.

Watch the speed increase and decrease. Your objective is to get the maximum speed, upwind. This is not the same as the maximum speed we can achieve in a straight line. Rather, it is the maximum speed actually achieved in the direction of our destination. Let us pretend our destination is more upwind than we can sail. The wind direction and speed may continually shift, sometimes frequently, sometimes but a little. Keep working your way upwind.

The concept we are working with is what sailors call "velocity made good to weather." This is related to your absolute speed through the water but corrected for the angle. If you have studied trigonometry, you can do the math. If your GPS can be set to an upwind destination and indicate the speed or time to that port, you can get a direct readout of your efforts to improve.

If that fails you, just imagine you are sailing, say, from Tampa to Key West, Florida, and the wind is out of the southwest. It is then directly on your nose or bow as you face your destination. You cannot sail there directly, but the greater the speed, and the lesser the angle from the wind, the sooner you will be sipping a cool one awaiting the sunset.

You will eventually learn to recognize slight changes in direction and speed of both the boat and the apparent wind. The apparent wind, the wind you feel, will change in direction for the following main reasons:

1. An actual change in direction of the wind.
2. An actual change in direction of the boat relative to the wind.
3. A change in velocity of the wind or of the boat. The velocity of the boat always shifts the apparent wind. As boat speed increases, this brings the

overall apparent wind more forward. If the wind dies, the same thing happens: the wind will seem to go forward and then die as the boat loses speed.

These things will be constantly happening. How will you know when to turn so the wind will fill the sails properly, yet not be stalled? Tomorrow we will refine our techniques using telltales. For today, just remember the rule from before: when in doubt, let it out. In this exercise, it is modified. When in doubt, turn the boat more toward the wind. If the sail starts to luff, turn the boat away from the wind until the sail just fills. It is better to have the sail luff occasionally than to sail with the sail always stalled.

Here are some tips to successful, faster upwind sailing:

1. The more you turn the rudder, the more it will drag in the water. That will slow the boat.
2. The neutral, or straight-ahead rudder position will vary depending on the amount of heel of the boat, the boat speed, the wind, and the waves. Finding the neutral position will enable you to steer left or right more accurately. If your tiller is not in the neutral position, your boat will drift to one side or the other. Since there is nothing equivalent to lane markings on the water, even experienced sailors will have some issue with this.
3. To assure the boat is heading in the generally correct direction, the helmsperson needs to check a compass or a distant fixed object.
4. A well-designed boat should have a balanced helm. This means that the tiller should require a slight pull to windward to keep the boat going straight.
5. If keeping the boat straight requires turning the rudder so far you might think the boat should be turning, you most likely have something to correct. Either the boat has something dragging in the water, or you have the boat heeling too much, or you need to change the size of the sails. Or perhaps the boat's design or rigging is a problem.

An upwind go-fast technique

There is always a better tack to be on when sailing upwind to a destination that cannot be reached on either tack alone. As the wind shifts, it will force you to sail further from your destination (a *header*, like heading them off at the pass) or help you by letting you point more toward it (a *lift*, lifting you up and carrying you to your destination). When you find a header, that header is a lift on the other tack. When a header persists, that is a good time to tack and take advantage of the lift to your destination. You will sail a shorter distance overall if you follow these persisting shifts. Racers know they must stay "in phase" with the shifts. There is no weather forecast that will tell you whether a header will last long enough to make it worth your while to tack. Only experience and attention will teach you that.

If the wind is a little off in one direction or another from your destination, one tack or the other will let you sail more directly to your destination. That tack is said to be favored. A tack can also be favored for other reasons: one direction will take you into a more favorable current, or out of an unfavorable one, or could take you to better winds or less waves.

Cruisers may find it worthwhile to head a little upwind of their destination. It is safer to give plenty of room from an obstruction. Doing this may eliminate some tacking.

A downwind go-fast technique

There is a related downwind go-fast technique. When sailing downwind, we do not need to head directly to our destination. Instead, we consider the variations in wind strength as we sail downwind. Downwind and upwind being relative terms, it can be considerably faster to sail a bit upwind of our destination, while the winds are relatively lighter. This adds our boat speed to the wind speed, helping us go a little faster. When the wind increases, we can head slightly downwind to compensate for the distance we sailed upwind. Any sailboat racer knows this rule as "Head up in the lulls and down in the puffs." Sometimes it is faster to sail relatively a bit upwind, then jibe and sail a bit upwind the opposite way, than to sail directly downwind to our destination. It will also increase the airflow across the deck, which can be much more comfortable on a warm, sunny day.

THE TENTH STEP: BOATING ETIQUETTE

Boating has its own etiquette.

The rules for guests are simple. Generally, do not question your captain, but bring to his attention safety issues that you think he may have overlooked. Bribe him instead with his favorite beverage. Bring your own food and drink, and share with the captain. Wear white-soled shoes. Clean them off before boarding. Do not be afraid to ask for a life jacket, or to ask how the radio works.

> *"Not to have control over the senses is like sailing in a rudderless ship, bound to break to pieces on coming in contact with the very first rock."*
>
> MAHATMA GANDHI

Figure 2.4. You can dress like a slob, but don't act like one by throwing things overboard. (Drawing by Clare Rosean)

If you've sailed on someone's boat in the previous summer and want to be regarded as a class act and increase your chances for another invitation, a good thing to do is offer to help prepare it in the spring for sailing. Even if you know nothing at all about boat maintenance, painting, or sanding, an offer to help out on the day of the mast-stepping or launching would be welcomed. Such a call to the owner should be timed for about a month before the season begins.

You may receive an offer to come to dinner or a drink at the local yacht club. There is no need to turn the invitation down; the clubs I have been to are low-key about joining. They will offer a membership but not press the issue.

Be sure you are moored so you will not interfere with others. Do not dock at the pump-out, the fuel dock, launch ramp, a dinghy dock, or in the vicinity of any crane. Move the boat and the trailer from the launch ramp as quickly as you can if anyone is waiting. Raise your mast at another location or before launching if vertical clearance—especially no wires!—permits, so you free up the launch ramp for others as soon as possible. Offer to help others as they approach the dock; offer to hold the mooring lines as they depart. Share information about local eateries and local hazards. Offer to take a new boater to your yacht club.

You are welcome to dress like a slob, but you may not act like one. Throw nothing overboard. Empty your porta-potty or holding tank only at approved locations. Avoid spilling fuel. Rinse off and dry your trailerable boat before going to another body of water to avoid spreading foreign invasive aquatic life. Do not ever throw or allow plastic to fall overboard; use reusable containers that stack when empty, such as Tupperware.

Smile and wave to your fellow sailors. You're sharing their fun.

Keep sailing!

BECOME A BETTER SAILOR:

Improve Your Sail Trim and Sailboating

Lake sailing (Photo courtesy Dan Waters)

The smoother the curve of the sail, the faster the boat

THE ELEVENTH STEP: TRIM SAILS FOR SPEED

Today, we will start to learn to maximize our boat speed in various weather conditions and begin to correct problems with the sails' shape. Then, we'll anchor and enjoy our lunch or dinner.

RESOURCES. Same as Day One, but with the addition of telltales, GPS, and inclinometer. Use telltales designed for a boat, or just get some yarn or strips of lightweight cloth and secure 6"- to 12"-lengths of it with some adhesive tape. Use the pattern shown in Figure 3.1 for the location of the tapes. An inclinometer is available at most boat-supply stores. It need not be elaborate or expensive. The most basic version will do. The GPS desired for this day is one that has the function of time to destination, or velocity made good to weather. You will select a destination in the "no-go" zone and tack as necessary to reach it, trying to increase your speed by adjustments to the sails and steering.

WHAT YOU WILL DO TODAY. Same as Days One and Two, but you will learn more details about sail adjustment.

In Days One and Two, we used only the most basic sail trim. It was a success. The boat moved at our command. Today, we will learn to fine trim our sails. To do this without memorization, we must learn how the sails move the

"When anyone asks how I can best describe my experience in nearly 40 years at sea, I merely say, uneventful. Of course there have been winter gales, and storms and fog and the like, but in all my experience, I have never been in any accident of any sort worth speaking about. . . . I never saw a wreck and never have been wrecked, nor was I ever in any predicament that threatened to end in disaster of any sort. You see, I am not very good material for a story . . . I cannot imagine any condition which would cause a ship to founder. I cannot conceive of any vital disaster happening to this vessel. Modern ship building has gone beyond that."

CAPTAIN EDWARD JOHN SMITH, COMMANDER OF THE *TITANIC*

Do not get overconfident!

boat. Newton's laws of motion govern all moving objects, sailboats included. A beauty of Newton's laws is their simplicity, so do not worry. Sail trim becomes only a little more complicated than speeding your bicycle up by pressing harder on the pedals. For those interested in the details, see Appendix F for a discussion on the physics of sail trim. This chapter contains the author's simplified explanation. The effort here is to provide a general guideline to sail trim. To trim your sails, you need to know what shape you are trying to create. To know what shape you are trying to create, it helps to know why a particular shape works. In other words, how does the sail move the boat?

The rules of the game can be stated in a few sentences. Allow the wind to flow smoothly along both sides of the sail. Have the sail shape a gentle curve so that the wind can follow the curve, because, if it does not, you have turbulence and wind eddies that do not help you go forward. Have a relatively flat rear half (*leech*) of the sail as discussed later in this chapter. Try to have the sails generate the most forward force with the least wind resistance, their greatest power-to-drag ratio. If the power of the sails is causing the boat to heel too much, reduce their power, especially toward the top of the sail (which, because of leverage against the tall mast, has more tilting effect).

How to know the wind is really moving correctly across the sail

We can see how the air is flowing by using the telltales attached on the sail. These small cloth strips will react to the airflow. If the airflow is smooth, they will be streaming smoothly against the sail. They may never be perfect, but try to get most of them to lie against the sail smoothly. Others at the leech (back edge) of the sail should stream straight outward, indicating a smooth flow as the wind on one side of the sail meets the wind from the other.

To go fast, use the telltales:

1. If the telltales at the top of the sail are luffing, but those on the bottom are okay, or vice-versa, the sail needs more or less twist.
2. To reduce twisting of the sail, make its sheet pull more downward. To increase twist, make its sheet pull less downward.
3. To make the jib sheet pull more or less downward, move its attachment to the boat forward or aft. There is a track on most boats to allow the point the sheet meets the boat, usually a block, to be moved. The traveler, moved in or out, or the vang, tightened or loosened, can change the twist on the mainsail.

Follow those simple rules. When the whole sail luffs, the telltales on both sides might misbehave. In that instance, you need to turn away from the wind until the sail fills.

Figure 3.1. (Drawing by Clare Rosean)

General guidelines of sail trim

There are some general guidelines to sail trim. Your sail will work best if it looks like the top half of an airplane wing.

The depth of the curve is proportionate to the power the sail can generate. Set the overall depth of the curve for the conditions: make the curve deeper for light winds, and flatten it for strong winds.

Look at the group of three illustrations in Figure 3.4 of the wind flowing along what we can call the outside of the sail. Notice how the wind is facing the sail. While not shown in the illustration, the wind on the inside of the sail is hitting with enough force to "inflate" it, filling the sail with wind and shaping it properly. If the wind strikes that side of the sail just right, it will flow along the inside of the sail, exerting a push on the sail.

The wind on the outside of the sail is particularly important. The wind on the outside of the sail is most effective if it strikes the outside front of the sail from the smallest angle possible. The greater the angle of the wind to the sail, the greater the likelihood of turbulence. So, the sail works best if the wind comes at it at a point just allowing the sail to inflate or fill. This makes it easier for the wind to follow the curve of the sail. This pulls on the sail, moving the boat. The wind on the outside of the sail is the most important force moving the boat forward. You can never make a boat sail well, except downwind, without engaging the wind outside the sail, causing it to flow as smoothly as possible along the sail.

This is why, as mentioned in Day One, regardless of the direction of the apparent wind relative to the boat, the apparent wind direction relative to the sail is kept constant! Your objective: let just enough wind on the inside of the sail to fill it.

The boats in Figure 3.2 going to the left are approaching the start. The boats going right will be starting later. Note that the boats going to the left of the picture are attempting to sail upwind as best as possible. The upwind boats have very tight, straight sails, as is required to sail at their best upwind. The boats sailing downwind have looser, more curved sails.

Figure 3.2. The start of the race to Mackinaw.

Figure 3.3. Nature abhors vacuum. (Drawing by Clare Rosean)

How the sails actually work

As the wind curves along the outside of the sail, it exerts a force. You can feel this force on the sheets when you set the sails. The sail will get much harder to pull in when the wind is pulling against it. This force is from the change in direction of the breeze caused by the airflow following the curve of the sail.

But how can this sail, which is just sitting there on the boat, propel a boat weighing tons forward? The answer is that the sail moves a lot of air. The typical illustrations in a how-to-sail book show only a small amount of air, right near the sail, being affected by the sail. But if you talk to those who have successfully raced sailboats, they can tell you how far away their boat is affected by the wind off another boat's sail. A boat's sail noticeably affects the wind hundreds of feet away. Many estimate the effect is significant at a distance seven times the height of the sail. So, as shown in Appendix F, the sail moves tons of air toward the rear of the boat. In turn, that propels the boat forward just as though it were a propeller pushing the air.

Returning to Figure 3.4, the illustration of wind being bent by a sail: Starting at top left it shows a curved line, commonly called an *airstream*. The air must remain near the sail. Otherwise there would be a vacuum between it and the sail, which nature abhors . . . the vacuum, that is, not the sail. We can think of the

Figure 3.4. (Drawing by Clare Rosean)

air moving along the sail as a stream, even though it is formed of tiny little molecules. Engineers often use the concept of airstreams for visualization purposes; we can, too.

At the top center, the next level of air, or airstream, across the sail is illustrated. The adjacent curved airstream must stay as close as it can to the first airstream. Otherwise, there would be a vacuum between the first airstream and the second.

On the last section, we see each adjacent curved line, a representation of an airstream, must stay next to its neighbor in turn, to avoid a vacuum. The curving effect diminishes very gradually. So, we don't have a tiny, narrow, airstream affected by the sail; we have tons of air at our command.

Shape and controls

Picture the smooth curve of your sail and all that air flowing past, changing direction more toward the stern of the boat as it goes across the sail, and you can see how we will make our sailboat move. It just requires us to get the wind smoothly flowing more in a direction toward the stern than it was before. Once we do that, nature takes over and sends more air in lockstep.

With time and experience, you will learn to make very slight adjustments to the sails. You will learn over time to adjust the sails for different wind conditions and to compensate for the rocking of the boat (more difficult in light winds).

Figure 3.5. Wind angle. (Drawing by Clare Rosean)

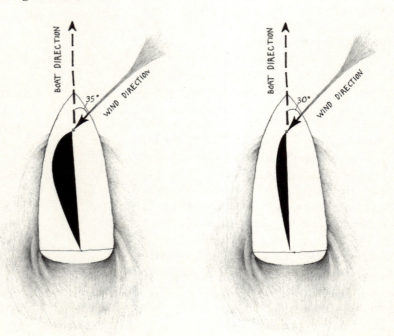

The more efficiently the sails bend the wind toward the rear, the better. If we flatten the sails there will be less curve of the sail, less wind bending, and less heeling force, so the boat will not tilt over as much. There is less force both forward and to the side. But, less bend or curve may be sufficient to move the boat forward if the wind is strong, and it may be a better compromise for safety and comfort. A flatter sail can fill at less of an angle from the wind, allowing the boat to head even more upwind (to windward), as in Figure 3.5. Sometimes, the boat actually moves faster with less sail area. It will be heeling less, the rudder will need to turn less, and the keel will be more straight down and stick deeper into the water, as you will see later in this chapter.

Put this into practice

A sail can be flattened by pulling on its various lines. Adjustments can also cause the top part to twist away from the wind, reducing its side force. Switch to a smaller sail for the stronger persisting winds. A smaller sail has less drag, so its power-to-drag ratio can be better than a larger, flattened sail. Sail area is always reduced for heavy-weather sailing.

When the wind is coming from behind the boat, it is no longer possible to get the same airplane wing–like shape as before. The sail twists. This is normal. On some boats, it is possible to adjust the lines to the point that the shape improves. A pole can be used to help shape the sail downwind.

Pulling the halyard tighter will flatten the sail by stretching the leading edge of the sail out. An airplane wing and a well-designed, well-set sail have the front part rounded. Make the deepest part of each sail's curve near the front of the sail, somewhere around 33 to 40 percent of the distance from the mast to the back of the sail (from luff to leech). This is known to be best because of wind tunnel tests on airplanes. Past that deepest point, the remaining two-thirds of a wing's surface is fairly flat and gets flatter. Scientists have studied wings, which they call *airfoils*, both theoretically and in wind tunnels for over a century. All successful airfoils, wings and sails, have this basic shape. The long, fairly straight section of the rear two-thirds or so exists so when the wind on one side meets the other, the airstreams will both continue more or less straight backwards instead of trying to push each other one way or another.

Sometimes you want to increase the tilt of the boat, and sometimes you want to decrease it. Decades ago, an article I read insightfully suggested sailing with a constant angle of heel. Within limits, this is an excellent concept. Sailboat designers know they must balance the forces, and a keelboat must heel sailing upwind. A good keelboat is designed to sail best at a certain angle of heel, usually around 15 to 20 degrees. Try to power up your sails to get to that angle of heel. Use crew weight to help get to the proper angle. Once the wind increases and you reach 20 degrees of heel, it is time to flatten sails, allow the tops to twist off, or reduce sail area. Crew weight moved to the high side will also reduce heel. This process can be fine-tuned. Using your GPS set to an upwind destination, watch as the speed made good to windward, or the time to your destination, changes. Fine-tuning the sails and the angle of heel, as well as becoming more subtle with the steering and sail trim, will give huge rewards in upwind sailing. It also is important when sailing upwind to have a well-designed sailboat, which is discussed in Day Seven.

If the sideways pull is too strong, the boat will heel more than it is designed to. This can slow the boat and be wet and uncomfortable. There are several reasons for this. As the sail leans outward with the tilt of the boat, its center of effort (the average location of its force) moves outward. It is like someone pulling on your outstretched arm, kept straight and stiff. That will make you, and the boat, want to turn. To correct that on your boat, you must turn the rudder to compensate. Turning the rudder increases its drag through the water. The boat's underwater shape, when tilted severely, may be less than optimal. The keel is no longer pointing straight down, so its effective depth is reduced.

The sail's angle to the wind is changed by moving it inward or outward, closer to or farther from the centerline of the boat. If the sail has an attachment to the boat that cannot be moved inward or outward past a certain point, try using a *barberhauler,* a line to pull the bottom rear corner (clew) in or out further, to see what that will do to boat speed in different conditions. Another limiting factor is the rig itself. A large, overlapping front sail (*genoa*) must be led out-side of the mast's supporting wires (shrouds). This limits the minimum angle to the wind.

The mainsail

Mainsails can have 1) a backstay adjuster (Figure 3.6). Other backstay adjusters on larger boats can be hydraulic and look like a bicycle pump with a lever to pump it. Backstay adjusters pull or loosen the backstay. Pulling on the backstay (or running backstay if so equipped) tightens the forestay, which can flatten the jib. It also tends to bend the mast. Bending the middle of the mast forward flattens the mainsail. We can also flatten the mainsail (see Figure 3.7) using 2) an outhaul, 3) a downhaul called a cunningham, or 4) the halyard, all of which may be adjusted to roughly equal tension. The outhaul, downhaul, and halyard controls flatten the front and bottom of the mainsail. Pulling the boom downward flattens the rear part (leech) of the triangular sail. The boom is pulled down or loosened with 5) a boom vang, and 6) the mainsheet (the line pulling on the boom, pulling on the mainsail). The mainsheet's angle can be adjusted by moving the point at which the sheet is attached to

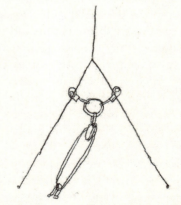

Figure 3.6. Backstay adjuster. The backstay tensioner can also tension the forestay, or bend the mast itself. (Drawing by Clare Rosean)

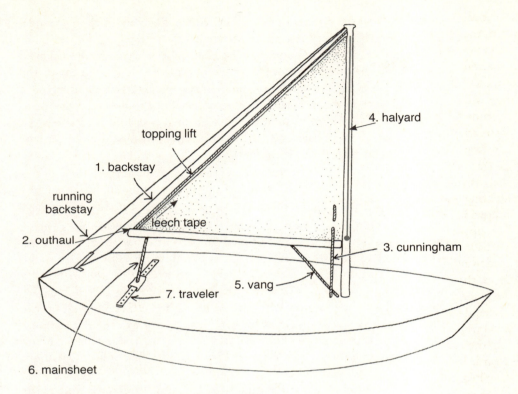

topping lift

1. backstay

running backstay

4. halyard

leech tape

2. outhaul

3. cunningham

7. traveler

5. vang

6. mainsheet

Figure 3.7. (Drawing by Christopher Hoyt)

the boat. The control for this is called 7) the traveler. Letting the traveler more downwind, more underneath the boom, allows the sheet to pull more downward. Adding tension to the sheet now flattens the main rather than bringing it in. The traveler can be moved even further out, this time moving the main outward. This will also reduce heeling. Also, the boat can be sailed a little more upwind than optimal. This is called *pinching* and can be a useful technique for dealing with a gust.

Except in extreme conditions, the mainsail is not replaced to reduce sail area but instead is shortened by the process called reefing. The mainsail can have none to as many as four reef points built into the sail. The main's halyard has to be loosened in the reefing process. These reef points can be operated in different ways. In common systems the front reef point may be hooked in at the boom or pulled in with a line and various lines used to tie down the rest of the sail. A final control you may use is a leech tape. This is a line that pulls the rear part of the sail tight. The leech tape keeps the rear of the sail from fluttering. Fluttering slows the boat and wears out the sail quickly.

DRILL. Try all the different methods of reducing heeling in various winds. Do this long before experiencing high winds.

While we are on the subject of the mainsail, some masts are weakened too much if the main is removed entirely while sailing with a jib alone. The mainsail limits the movement of the mast, especially its freedom to move back and forth in the middle. This movement, if not controlled, can lead to failure of the mast itself. A mast that lacks strong wires limiting its freedom in mid-mast to move back and forth should never be sailed with a jib alone, because the jib adds to the stress on the mast.

The slot

There is a gap between the jib and the main, called the *slot*. The jib hurtles air aft to the main. The effect is much like a set of flaps on an airplane wing. Flaps can provide an additional 50 percent or more lift on a wing. The trick is to keep the slot open so air can flow through it. Generally, to set the air flow through the slot, set the jib first. With the air flowing across the jib nicely, experiment with the mainsail trim. It is possible to have the boat moving best with a little bit of jib-induced luffing on the main, but more likely this is not the case. Just be aware of the slot's importance as you experiment with the sail trim on your boat. For a detailed look at wing configurations, see *Theory of Wing Sections*, (Abbot and Doenhoff, Dover Publications, 1959).

Continue to sail, experimenting with sail trim. Watch for wind shifts and weather changes. Concentrate on increasing boat speed, or just watch the scenery and wave to your fellow sailors. You are one of them now.

THE TWELFTH STEP: CREW OVERBOARD PROCEDURES

The shout "man overboard!" is being replaced with "crew overboard!".

Do you remember the warning from Day One, "don't pee overboard"? Don't laugh about that. I've been told scary statistics about how many drowning victims have their flies open.

If someone else does fall overboard, scream, "CREW OVER-BOARD!" and throw a flotation device at him immediately. Try to actually hit his hand with it. It is the job of immediate, highest, and only priority of everyone aboard to rescue that crew. His fly can be zipped later. Everyone should be on deck ASAP. One person should keep his eyes on the victim and point an arm at him at all times AND DO NO OTHER JOB. THAT IS THE MOST IMPORTANT JOB. IT DOES NO GOOD TO

TURN THE BOAT ABOUT QUICKLY IF SIGHT OF THE VICTIM IS LOST. IF SIGHT IS LOST, THE VICTIM IS LOST. If there are two or more aboard, YOU AS THE LEAST EXPERIENCED CREW WILL HAVE THAT MOST IMPORTANT JOB. DO IT WELL. Do not turn away from him for even an instant. Continuously point at him. Do not allow yourself to be distracted from this job. If anyone asks you a question, do not turn. Instead, while continuing to look and point in the direction of the victim, answer with a shout loud enough for everyone behind you to hear you. The boat must be turned around by the quickest means. Keep pointing as the boat is turning. If you are the only one on deck, you must, without ever looking away, stop the boat and turn it back toward the victim. If there is a ship to shore (marine) radio, grab it, face the victim, and make your mayday call.

If you are alone on deck, and there are others below, the order in which you do things is as follows:

1. Turn and point to the victim.
2. Scream "crew overboard!".
3. Throw the crew-overboard pole and flotation devices, whatever there is within reach.
4. Start to return the boat to the victim.
5. Repeat screaming "crew overboard!" until crew below responds.
6. Place a mayday call unless you are confident you will recover the victim without assistance. Once the crew is recovered, get on the radio to tell all you have cancelled the mayday.

Deal with the sails as necessary. It is better to arrive under sail than under power, because the propeller can kill, and it is better to approach the victim with the boat to leeward (the wind passes the victim before reaching the boat), but get to the victim as quickly as possible. Once the victim is close enough that the crew cannot possibly lose sight of him, the person pointing can be released to other duties, such as getting a boarding ladder or some line to hoist him or help him climb aboard. Be aware the boat must be stopped to get the victim aboard. It is very hard work and requires a lot of strength to hoist a crew aboard. If the boat is moving, it is much more difficult. If the boat has equipment (such as the popular Lifesling™) designed for recovery of crew, use it. Sometimes a halyard can be tied around the crewmember, who can then be winched aboard. Another technique is to drop the mainsail in the water and slide it beneath the unfortunate crewmember. Hoisting the main will then also hoist the victim. No other crewmember should enter the water to help out the victim, unless it is the only possible way to save a life, and all of the following conditions exist: the volunteer is a great swimmer (perhaps a lifeguard); the volunteer is tethered to the boat (but a regular tether is too short; use a line instead); a swim ladder is present so the rescuer can get aboard again; the job can be done without encountering hypothermia; and enough crew remain to hoist both the victim and volunteer aboard.

It is good practice to perform a crew-overboard drill from time to time. Just throw a spare cushion or life jacket and steer to return to it. As you gain experience, you will want to learn maneuvers specific to recovering a crew overboard. They are all designed to stop and reverse the boat's course as quickly as possible. Until one maneuver is found to be best, I am in favor of just turning around ASAP with whatever maneuver you can make the quickest.

THE THIRTEENTH STEP: ANCHORING

The two fundamentals in anchoring are having the correct equipment and using it properly. First, we'll discuss the equipment.

The size and type of anchor you need is determined mainly by the size of the boat, but also by the type of bottom and the wind and water conditions to be experienced. A great guide to the type of anchor is what people in your local area rely upon but sized for your boat and the conditions you will want to anchor in. The anchor manufacturers' Internet sites will tell you if your existing equipment is sized correctly for your boat. While it is good to get the size recommended for your size boat, even larger is better. Best is to get the largest you can handle, because it will have a better chance of holding your boat if conditions get worse.

Any anchor should be connected directly to chain. The chain length and weight should be as the anchor manufacturer recommends, but at least one-half the boat length. After that length of chain, the anchor line (rode) can be rope or chain. An all-chain rode is desirable for several reasons. When anchoring in rocky areas, chain is more resistant to cutting and abrasion than rope. The additional chain weight helps make the pull more horizontal; it can lie on the bottom, and the force to lift it off the bottom acts a bit like a spring, absorbing the shock loads. However, an all-chain rode is going to be very heavy, and an electric winch (windlass) will be necessary. It is no longer recommended to use stainless steel as rode. *Practical Sailor's* tests showed stainless-steel rode is more susceptible to failure without warning than other types.

Each part of the anchoring equipment, which is called *ground tackle*, must be properly secured together. This mandates frequent inspections for wear and tear and *electrolysis*, which occurs whenever dissimilar metals are in proximity.

When anchoring, it is advisable to let out rode equal to seven times the distance from the bottom of the sea or lake to the boat deck.

Put length markings on the rode. This will help ensure enough scope has been let out. A distinctive mark every 20 feet will suffice. Too many marks means too much counting and calculating. If you use a windlass, be sure whatever marking method you utilize will not foul it. As a suggestion, if using chain, paint one link at 20 feet; paint two adjacent links at 40 feet, etc. You will have a clue even if you lose count. Other marking systems involve weaving ribbons at differing distances from the anchor. This is particularly easy to do with three-strand nylon rode.

If using a windlass, or an all-chain rode, your anchoring equipment should also include a *snubber*, which is a strong but stretchable rope to connect the rode to your strongest cleat. This reduces strain on both the boat and the windlass. Once the snubber is attached, the strain on the windlass is eliminated by letting out some chain.

In rocky areas, or areas with debris on the bottom, a *trip line* can be rigged. This attaches to the bottom of the anchor, must be a little longer than the depth of the water, and must be attached to a float. If the anchor gets trapped, the trip line can be picked up and the anchor hauled out the opposite way it came in. The trip line can be of a lesser diameter than the rode, since it doesn't have to hold the boat.

SUGGESTED HAND SIGNALS

Waving a hand above one's head in a circle means "speed up." A hand pointed straight down means "stop." An open hand in a direction means "go that way." A single finger pointed asks "do you see that?" A fist aimed in a direction means "danger that way." Pumping a hand on chest means "lower or raise the anchor."

Do you need a bridle?

Catamarans will require a *bridle*, a simple strong line to connect the two bows to the anchor's rode. With the anchor rode in the middle of the bridle, a triangle is formed. This both spreads the load on both bows and centers the anchoring force so the bows are aligned with the wind. (Also, if it becomes desirable, the bridle can be shifted so that the bows are pointed a slight angle from the wind and waves. This possibly can result in a smoother ride.)

Hand signals

The anchoring procedure begins with agreeing on hand signals. It may be very difficult for the person steering to hear the person on the bow handling the anchor. Hand signals should include stop, go, left, right, a signal for danger in such and such direction, lower anchor, and raise anchor. The signals agreed upon should require one hand only, so the other can be used to hold on or steer. Secure the extreme end of the rode to the boat. Select a spot to anchor in.

Consider that the anchor may drag, especially if the wind or current shifts in direction. So, if anchoring overnight, you must select a spot that allows for the boat to swing in a circle greater than the length of the rode in all directions without causing a collision or the boat to run aground. If you are just stopping for a while and will have someone on board, you need only allow enough room to let you raise anchor to get away before an impact, if the anchor drags. Never anchor among coral.

Lowering the anchor

Once you have selected a spot, approach it with the bow pointed, as nearly as practicable, into the wind. This will better allow you to judge your final position after setting the anchor.

Singlehanders may choose to anchor by the stern and, once anchored, tie the rode to the bow, then untie it from the stern. This requires leaving enough rode to take the anchor rode to the bow while the rode remains tied to the stern.

The anchor should be lowered, not dropped or thrown, when the boat speed is nil. Let the boat back slowly downwind to allow the anchor to set. If you have an engine, putting it in reverse at a modest thrust will help set the anchor. Make sure you do not let your rode, or any other line, near your propeller or propeller shaft. Then, only after the boat has stopped moving, increase thrust to test the set.

Check your position by comparing the direction and distance of fixed objects. If that changes more than a wind shift can account for, your anchor is dragging and must be reset. Perform frequent anchor checks by comparing your position as before. This means you do not get to sleep straight through the night. The frequency of your anchor checks depends upon your familiarity with the boat, the anchor, the *holding ground*, which is the nature of the bottom, as well as the wind and water state. If your GPS has an anchor alarm warning that you are drifting, so much the better.

Be aware of reversing tides and substantial wind shifts. A wind shift or change in the direction of the tide may pull your anchor out of the bottom and cause even a well-set anchor to drag.

Courtesy at anchorages

When anchoring, choose a spot as far from other boats as necessary to give others the most privacy you can. Before finalizing that choice, estimate as best you can the effect of any wind shifts. To do so, estimate the amount of scope each nearby boat has on their anchor rode and visualize it turning in the wind, pivoting from the anchor. Consider, too, that anyone's anchor may drag. Remember, too, that an all-chain rode will cause the boat to turn more slowly than rope rode when the wind shifts. The last person to anchor is the first to have to move under etiquette rules at anchorages if conditions require.

Only in a crowded anchorage should you be anywhere near another boat. Be sure your anchor will not cross another boat's anchor or rode even if the wind shifts or your anchor drags a bit. Avoid anchoring near any improperly anchored boat. If the other's rode doesn't show the proper scope, assume it is improperly anchored. Only in the absence of enough wind to stretch the rode out might a boat without sufficient apparent scope be properly anchored. In that event, all boats nearby will show little scope, and you must assume the moment the breeze comes up, the boats will move away from their anchors.

If you wish to play loud music, go to the edge of the anchorage as far from others as possible. Respect your neighbors' desire for peace.

If you see another boat dragging anchor, or banging into the dock, can you spare an anchor, or a fender?

Maybe you should dinghy over to a nearby boat and offer some of your food and beverages.

What will you do now that you are anchored? How will you pass the time? That could be the subject of another book . . . I'll leave that to you. Perhaps you will learn to tie a bowline . . .

THE FOURTEENTH STEP: LARGER BOATS; THE CLOVE HITCH AND THE BOWLINE, THE "KING OF KNOTS"

The Clove Hitch is another easy knot. Its advantage over the other knots is it can be tied easily, and it immediately sets the length of line beyond the knot. It is perfect to tie fenders to a rail or lifeline. It is not as secure as the Bowline, so it must not be used to tie the boat to the dock or tie sheets to sails. It consists of only two loops.

First, the now familiar loop to the left is formed, Figures 3.8 and 3.9. It looks a little different from the others, because it is vertical.

Figure 3.8. First loop.

Figure 3.9a. Continue with the second loop. This loop is in the same direction as the first loop, but is on the other side of the main part of the line.

Figure 3.9b. Cinch it up and you are done.

The Bowline (*bo-lin*), used on larger boats, is a challenge to the beginner. It is called the "king of knots" for good reason. It is strong yet can be released easily. Once learned, it is simple to tie. While there are better knots for some specialized uses, a Bowline can be used for almost any purpose. Only a few of those specialized knots are used with any regularity, and sailors get by with just the four knots taught here.

First, the now familiar loop is formed, Figure 3.10. As in the Stopper Knot, Cleat Hitch, and Clove Hitch we begin by taking a turn to the left to form the loop.

Continue extending the working part around in a circle, forming a second loop, Figure 3.11.

Figure 3.10.

Figure 3.11.

The working part enters the first loop formed, so we now have two loops, Figure 3.12. Notice how the line goes into the loop from underneath and comes out on top.

Notice the line escapes the loop by going over it, and then underneath the main part of the line, Figure 3.13.

In Figure 3.14, can you see what this step was? We just shoved the line back into the loop again, going over one part of the loop, and then back under the loop and out. We've just passed the working part through the same loop hole our line had exited just before. Just like a two-lane highway, it went on the same route through the loop but in the opposite direction. A common memory device describing the knot from the point the second loop

Figure 3.12.

Figure 3.13.

Figure 3.14.

Figure 3.15.

is formed is "the rabbit comes out the hole (Figure 3.12), goes around the tree (Figure 3.13), and goes back in the hole (Figure 3.14)."

The completed Bowline is cinched up tight. This requires pulling each portion tight several times until each part is at least as tight as in Figure 3.15.

On the next rainy day, practice making this knot. Keep practicing until you can tie them without referring to the instructions.

When do I use a Bowline?

The king of knots can be used to tie two lines together, to tie a mooring line to any attachment on a pier, to tie a halyard or sheet to a sail, to tie fenders to the boat, or to tie any line to anything that you want to attach securely yet be able to release easily. Its only weaknesses are that it can release accidentally from a flailing sail, especially if not cinched up tight, and that it is difficult to release if the line is under tension. It is released by pulling out its cinched-up sections in the opposite manner it was cinched up.

THE FIFTEENTH STEP: LARGER BOATS; WINCHES AND FURLING GEAR

Larger boats, typically over 20 feet, have winches with separate handles to help you raise, lower, and control the sails. Because this varies from boat to boat, it's easiest to have someone show you which line gets led where. The person who sold, lent, or accompanied you on the boat will do this and will check out the boat for safety. You can do it on your own. The following photographs show typical hardware for the lines controlling the sails. Compare these to the boat you are on.

Following are photos of winches. The winch's outer surface is called the *drum*. Ratchets inside allow the drum to move only clockwise. Usually the winches are near the cockpit or on the cabin top. Sometimes winches are found on the mast,

Figure 3.16.

to help hoist the sails. The winch in Figure 3.16 is *self-tailing*. The portion of the sheet coming out of the winch after being pulled around the winch is called the *tail*, like the tail of an animal. If the winch is not self-tailing, someone must keep tension on the tail so the line does not slip along the durm. As in the photo, after wrapping the line around the drum several times the line is led over the silver prong at left near the top of the drum and into the jaws, the black feature at the top of the drum. Feeding the line into the jaws the rest of the way around will trap the line, holding it for you. Once the line is adjusted to the proper tension, it may be secured with a nearby cleat. This can allow the line to be released from the winch so the winch can be used on another line.

The line is wrapped around the winch, *always clockwise*. The winch handle acts like a

THE WINCH

A winch always requires the rope to be wrapped around it several times, always in a clockwise direction. The rope must be tight on the winch, because the winch relies on friction between the rope and the winch's drum.

lever on the line, giving the crew an advantage much like a tire jack lifts an entire car. Do not lose the winch handle. Make sure it is completely inserted into the winch when in use and stowed properly when not in actual use.

The procedure for using a winch is: Make a single clockwise wrap around the winch with the line. Then, pull on it by hand—it is faster than winching—until the load gets to be too much to pull the line in. In Figure 3.17, notice that the portion of the sheet at the bottom of the photo is not slack. It is being held by a crew member keeping tension. Take additional wraps around the winch as needed. The more wraps around the winch, and the more tension on the tail, the more friction the winch has on the line. Add two more wraps around the winch (a total of three), plus add one wrap for every 10 feet of boat length above 20 feet. So try four wraps for a 30-foot boat. In lighter winds, as when the photo was taken, two wraps were sufficient. In stronger winds, you may need to fill the entire outer surface of the winch's drum to get sufficient friction. Without enough wraps and tension, it will be like a car's drive wheels spinning on snow. There would be insufficient friction to get the job done.

Never forget the two most important rules: keep your hands in a safe position (so they cannot get trapped even if a line moves suddenly), and keep yourself securely on the boat (be particularly careful if you are using both your hands in operating a winch).

Figure 3.17.

Put your winch handle into the socket on the very top of the winch and crank away. The winch may have a transmission like a car or bicycle does, giving it two or (rarely) three speeds. A high speed lets you pull the sheet in quickly. Lower speeds give you more leverage, so it is easier to crank, just like it is easier to pedal a bicycle in a lower gear. Gears are changed by reversing the direction the handle is being cranked in. Otherwise, always crank clockwise. Once the position of the sail is set, the line can be secured in a cleat.

The line can jam on the winch if the tail is not pulled straight out. Be sure if you handle the tail you are not pulling upward or downward on the line. Doing so can cause one part of the line to jam tightly against another (see Figure 3.18).

A means to fix that is shown in Figure 3.19 (next page), where the winch handle is used for leverage to pull out an override too tight to pull out with your hands alone.

If a lot of line comes off the winch, then both hands will be needed for tailing, so that one hand can hold it tight while the other finds a new location to hold the line. If the person cranking is also handling the tail, it will be necessary to pause cranking while the grip on the line is switched.

To *sheet out,* just remove the line from the cleat (or the self-tailing device if so equipped, see below) and let the line out. It is not required, nor is it desirable, to completely remove the line from the winch to sheet out.

Figure 3.18.

Figure 3.19.

CAUTION

If you release a line under tension, be very careful not to get your hands caught. Hold the line with both hands, and ease it slowly. If it is urgent to release the line, release it quickly, and make sure your hands are safe from rope burn or getting caught.

One or more wraps can be removed to make it easier to sheet out, but the winch takes a lot of the strain off the crew, more strain than most people can handle.

Some winches reverse direction, so the line can be eased without removing it from the winch. At this writing that is not common. There are also electric winches available. Be especially careful to keep your hands clear of an electric winch.

Furling gear

Even smaller boats can have a furling jib. If it is a furling jib, it is particularly easy to set. It is easiest to unfurl it by winching in the jib sheet with a little wind pressure on the sail. Unless the gear manufacturer states otherwise, it is best to furl or unfurl it on a *beam* reach, with the wind off the side of the boat. You could reduce pressure on the sail by blanketing it, using the main to block some of the wind from the jib. You can use blanketing as a racing tactic some day; instead of blanketing your own sail, you blanket your opponent's.

An example of jib furling gear is shown in Figure 3.20. Pulling the line outward spins the base, which winds the sail in above it. Pulling the jib sheets out unwinds the sail. The jib can be pulled in or out either fully or partially as desired. The furling line is usually led the length of the boat all the way to the cockpit. When winding the sail, some tension must be

Figure 3.20.

maintained on the sheet. When unwinding, some tension must be maintained on the furling line.

THE SIXTEENTH STEP: LARGER BOATS; MANEUVERING WITH THE ENGINE

Consistent with the objective of learning to sail, our engine discussion is limited to maneuvering in the harbor.

Engine operation varies, but all engines must be started in neutral gear. Unlike your car, there may be no interlock, and your engine can be, but should not be, started in gear. Have someone teach you the starting procedure for your particular engine. If it is a gas engine, first check for gas fumes on deck, in the cabin, in the engine area and operate the blower for several minutes. See that any portable tank is connected and the outboard lowered into the water. There may be a choke to pull out before starting. The throttle should be just slightly opened. Start the engine with the pull rope, key, or starter button. Once it starts, push the choke closed. Check that cooling water is coming out.

WIND AND CURRENT

Whether under sail or power, whether actually docking or just travelling to or from the dock in any narrow channel or crowded area, be aware that wind and current will move the boat around and affect your speed and direction of travel. Determine the current and wind directions and learn to anticipate their effects on the boat. To compensate, you will point the boat a bit into the wind or current.

Leaving the dock under power just requires looking in the direction of travel to verify the path is clear and, often, backing out. Steering while backing has its difficulties. The boat may respond sluggishly to the rudder, and the rudder may be difficult to hold at the chosen angle.

It is good practice to back up only as absolutely necessary. If the engine is in forward gear, reverse gear then can act as a brake, and vice versa. Be sure your engine is at its lowest possible speed when switching between for-

SINGLEHANDING

When singlehanding, before leaving the dock it is possible to put the engine in gear and release all dock lines but one, which should be in easy reach. The one dock line is placed under tension with the engine's thrust holding the boat in place. Reduce engine speed until the line can be released, and promptly move away from the piers.

ward, neutral, and reverse. Be careful: make certain the outboard's interlock will keep the outboard from tilting up in reverse. Interlock failure can be dangerous. Note also that accelerating the engine in either forward or reverse will have a side effect not seen on land. It will turn the boat a bit. This varies from boat to boat. Anticipate this, and learn.

When returning to the dock, if possible approach heading into the wind so the wind will act as a bit of a brake.

DOCKING. At whatever location you dock, you will use several fenders and at least four dock lines. In the event you need more than four dock lines, you may use other lines, such as jib sheets, provided you will not be docking with your sheets for any extended period.

A typical fender arrangement for a small sailboat was shown in Figure 1.32. A larger boat will need more fenders. Typically you will want the largest fenders for pleasure boats that will fit in the storage area available. I prefer round or cylindrical fenders hung vertically. They rotate rather than scrape the hull. They must be equipped with the largest diameter lines that fit and be long enough to touch the water, if necessary. A typical dock-line arrangement was shown in Day One (see Figure 1.32).

Sometimes it is necessary to orient the fenders horizontally. This is the case if a vertical pole sticks out from the dock. A vertical fender is likely to roll off of a vertical pole. A fender board will help protect the boat from striking a vertical pole. Round fenders can be connected to form a long horizontal string when advisable.

If it is possible to attach lines to the other side of the dock (without interfering with other boats or blocking another boat's potential space), do so.

Commercially available dock lines with an eye splice already made can be purchased in lengths as short as 15 feet and are generally available in five-foot increments (e.g., 20 feet, 25 feet) in ⅜-, ½-, and ¾-inch diameters. For dock lines, I prefer the cheaper three-strand line, because it tends to stretch more. Its handling characteristics are fine for docking. Be sure the line diameter is right for your boat; the largest to fit your cleats is best. You may also want a section of stretchy rubber, called a snubber, to reduce the stress on the boat as it reaches the end of its rope.

What about the tide, or other changes in the depth? If the dock you tie to floats, this is less of a worry. If the dock is fixed in height, in a tidal zone your lines need to be long enough to allow for the boat to rise and sink. It is best to connect the lines to farther away points than one would normally. This would allow more length for the boat to rise and fall in the tides, while holding it close to the dock. Seek advice from locals in dealing with extreme conditions in the particular harbor.

THE SEVENTEENTH STEP: LARGER BOATS; MARINE TWO-WAY RADIO

The marine radio is the best way to seek help in an emergency. If, and only if, your emergency is life-threatening, begin with the words, "Mayday, Mayday, Mayday" followed by, for example, "We are sinking," or "We have a life-threatening medical emergency." If, and only if, your emergency threatens serious harm to the vessel, but is not life-threatening, begin with the words, "Pan-Pan, Pan-Pan, Pan-Pan" (actually pronounced *Pahn-Pahn*), followed by, for example, "We have lost our mast and rudder and need assistance." And if it is an essential navigation or safety issue, you may begin with the words, "Securité, Securité, Securité" (actually pronounced *Securitay*), followed by, for example, "Our rudder is damaged, and we have poor maneuverability. We are entering ___harbor in two minutes. All concerned traffic is requested to please stay clear." As soon as you are done speaking, release the microphone button—otherwise, your radio will not receive any replies. Wait 30 seconds to listen for a response. Then, repeat your pan-pan or mayday call. Never use the radio just to chat.

Once the emergency is resolved, send, "Cancel [Pan-Pan, Mayday], Cancel [Pan-Pan, Mayday]. This is [boat name]. [Doctor now on board]; [patient stable]; or [in safe harbor, as applicable.] Standing by on 16. Out."

If you are calling for directions in a harbor, or to call a bridge, look up the channel number the harbormaster or bridge monitors. It will be on your chart or cruising guide. If you are calling another vessel, try channel 9 first. Avoid the use of 16 except as absolutely necessary or in emergencies. Once you reach a boater on 9 or 16, switch to an open (not in use) ship-to-ship channel such as 68, 69, 71, or 72. When you finish your brief conversation, say clearly, "This is [boat name] clearing channel ___ and standing by on 16."

4 BECOMING A SELF-RELIANT SAILOR

"There is nothing—absolutely nothing—half so much worth doing as simply messing about in boats."

KENNETH GRAHAME, *THE WIND IN THE WILLOWS*

THE EIGHTEENTH STEP: INSPECT YOUR BOAT

On this day you will inspect your boat yourself. These inspections are to be done at least annually, and before any substantial voyage. This will help you to anticipate, eliminate, or learn how to deal with problems that may arise someday.

A responsible attitude

Safety is paramount. Follow the rule that anything that goes wrong is the fault of the skipper—you. Your attitude is to be one of complete responsibility. If you do not know how to perform the various inspections and repairs, it is your job as captain to get someone competent to do this.

The maintenance suggestions in Appendix E assume you will either sail on that boat regularly, or you will be sailing in a location or to such a distance that you cannot count on immediate help. They may be considered overkill if you are sailing on a millpond, in waist-deep water. An effort has been made to cover the most important points for the non-owner. A pre-purchase inspection includes all of these points and much more. Before

Figure 4.1. (Photo courtesy UK Sailmakers)

purchasing any but the simplest of dinghies, a professional marine survey and consultation with someone knowledgeable who is not interested in the outcome is highly recommended. Ask the surveyor for advice on maintenance of your specific model, in particular with regard to the keel and rudder attachments.

Your small and simple boat will be simple to inspect. We will start with the basic small boat and move on to inspecting larger boats.

The rig

Many dinghies have no wires supporting the mast. In those cases, check the mast step for cracks and debris. In Sunfish and Lasers the maststep is just a round hole in the deck. Debris or sand in the hole or on the bottom of the mast will degrade the integrity of that hole rapidly. Check also for cleanliness and general condition.

Shrouds, stays, and their connections

Most boats have wires holding up the mast. The ones in front and back are called *stays*. The ones to the side are called *shrouds*. Look at all the wires supporting the mast. With your small boat, you should also be able to lower the mast and examine the fittings at its top. If lowering the mast for inspection is impractical, use binoculars to see the wires and their connections high up. Are any wires unwound or bent even slightly? Check the end fittings within reach and near deck level with a magnifying glass. Look for any hairline cracks. Also, run your fingers along each fitting and wire within reach. Do the same with the lines. If you spot any damage or corrosion, or unwound wires, replace the fitting(s) and accompanying wires immediately. Make sure each fitting is secured and is complete with a clevis and cotter pin or ring (Figure 4.2). The cotter pins should be taped over to prevent damage to sails or cuts

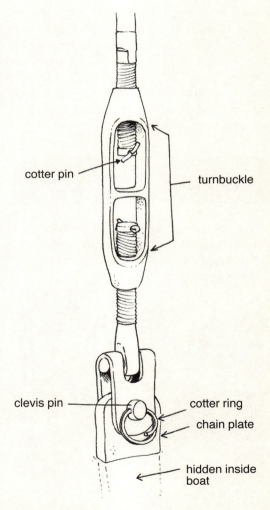

Figure 4.2. (Drawing by Christopher Hoyt)

to the crew. Check the *chainplates*. These are the important structural fittings that tie the hull itself to the wires holding up the mast. The larger and most important part of the chainplate is usually below the deck and may be hidden from view (Figure 4.2). Have yours evaluated by an expert.

Running rigging

Running rigging refers to all of the sheets, halyards, and other lines that raise, lower, and adjust the sails. Check for wear and fraying on these lines. Note that on your small boat, the lines are usually larger and stronger than they need be, in order to be thick enough for ease in handling. This gives extra safety not necessarily found on larger boats.

STAPLE REMOVER

You will run across cotter rings. An excellent tool to hold and spread the ring apart for placing and removing them is a staple remover

Figure 4.3.

The hull

Check the fiberglass for cracks. Small spider-web cracks may indicate only flexing, which may not be a problem but should be evaluated. A fiberglass hull will outlast us all with only minor maintenance. Check that all fastenings are secured. All cleats and running rigging fittings should be held to the fiberglass with bolts through strong backing plates.

Check the attachments for the rudder. Check for cracks and wear on the centerboard and rudder.

Openings in the hull are a particular concern. A large boat will have two for each engine, at least one for each head and sink and for some other accessories, some below the waterline, some barely above. These should be frequently inspected. Typically, the through-hull fitting connects to a hose. The through-hull fitting should include a seacock, with a lever to quickly shut off the flow of water when necessary. The seacocks require routine maintenance, usually including lubrication while the boat is on dry land and occasionally exercising the shut-off lever. Each end of the hose should have two stainless-steel hose clamps securing it. Many hoses must have a vented loop, really a half turn above the waterline. Each through-hull should have secured nearby a plug to fill the hole if something breaks.

Sails and equipment

Pull out the sails you will be using. Look for frayed, loose, or torn stitching. Pull on any suspect areas as hard as you can. Have them evaluated and repaired as necessary by a sailmaker as soon as you can. Minor fraying shouldn't be a problem in the mild winds we will sail in, because your sails have been out in worse and aren't ripped.

Figure 4.4. (Photo courtesy UK Sailmakers)

As you improve your sailing, someday you may want to take pictures of your sails in action to show to and consult with your sailmaker or just an experienced sailor. Your sailmaker will be able to tell from the pictures which sails he might want to recut to perform better. An experienced sailor might help you with sail trim issues. Be sure you can tell them the conditions the photo was taken in, such as apparent wind direction, wind speed, and angle of heel.

Make sure all required safety equipment is present. Check the flares: are they out of date? When you seek a radio check, do it on channel 9, not 16. Check the navigation lights and all electronics. You cannot sail at night without functioning navigation lights. Have towels and blankets to dry and warm wet crew. If you have fuel on board, you need at least one fire extinguisher. The Coast Guard has rules for how many you may need depending on the type and size of boat and engine.

ADDITIONAL STEPS FOR LARGER BOATS

Learn about your boat's systems.

Engine systems

Become familiar with the sounds the engine makes at various speeds. If the sound changes, that may be your first and only warning of difficulty. "Check engine" lights such as in your car aren't found on boats. A change in sound and a sluggish boat may simply mean weeds have clogged the propeller. Read the engine manual. The engine manual will tell you among other things how to check the fuel flow, the ignition system, spark plugs, lubrication, and coolant. Every time you start the engine, or the sound changes, make sure cooling water is flowing. Usually, this can be seen coming out of the exhaust system.

If you sail in salty or dirty water, flush the engine after each use with fresh, clear water per the owner's manual.

Write down the specific oil, oil filter, and spark plugs you will need to have aboard. Locate what spares are aboard; add whatever you may need.

If your engine has a steady, uninterrupted fuel supply, coolant, lubrication, and reliable ignition (in the case of a gas engine), it will continue to run.

Check the fuel tank. Are there rust spots? Is there gunk or water at the bottom of the tank? That will find its way to the fuel intake and the engine at the worst possible time, when the tank is stirred by rough water. The tank bottom can be cleared and fuel can be "polished" with the proper equipment. Are the fittings dry, or do they show evidence of leaks? What about the tank itself? Any leak needs to be corrected. Any rusty fitting should be cleaned or replaced. Check for worn hoses. Check the connections at the engine and fuel filters. Is the fuel fresh? Is there enough fuel to see you through your present cruising plans? Fill it today as necessary, but remember that you will want the fuel to stay fresh, so do not put a season's supply aboard.

Check the oil. Remember that if your outboard is an older two-cycle engine, the fuel must be mixed with oil in the proper ratio (usually 50 parts gas to one part oil). A four-cycle engine has crankcase oil like your car. Is it at the proper level on the dipstick? Does it look dirty? Does it look milky? Has the oil been changed recently? The manual will tell you how often the oil needs to be changed, but in general, seasonal sailors have the oil and filter changed at the time the boat is hauled out in the fall. Milky oil is a potentially serious issue. It means water is mixing with the oil. This can be caused by a serious engine problem and will lead to engine failure. Immediate service is recommended. (If it is your boat and you are in doubt about the age or condition of the oil, pump out the old oil and replace it, disposing of the used oil in an environmentally sound manner.)

Does the engine seem to overheat? Engine overheating issues are almost certainly coolant issues if the engine revs properly and the propeller can drive the boat at normal speeds. From time to time, check that cooling water is leaving the engine. Outboards have cooling water coming out from higher on the engine. A rubber impeller is all that is pushing the water around. Those seem to last only a year or two in a boat, even though they last a car's lifetime.

If the engine does not reach the proper operating *rpms*, this can cause poor fuel economy, overheating, reduced speeds, poor battery charging, and shortened engine life. The manufacturer's website will tell you your engine's optimal shaft speed for maximum horsepower. Two advantages of outboard engines come into play. The outboard propeller and lower unit can be raised out of the water when sailing, reducing drag, and can be inspected and cleared of lines, etc. without difficulty. However, you will not be able to determine engine rpms without a tachometer. Most small outboards lack tachometers.

Does the boat have a propane cooking or heating system? A propane system could have been added by an amateur. Check to see that the propane bottle is firmly attached to the hull. Make sure it is in a dedicated location such that any propane gas spills or leaks (which are extremely dangerous, because propane is heavier than air and can collect in the hull or cabin, awaiting a chance to explode) will instead drain overboard.

European-built boats may be built to a different standard and might not have this feature. Regardless of the design, test for propane leaks. Pressurize the system by opening the main valve, with all the valves at the propane-powered items shut. Then, close the main valve again. If there is any decrease in pressure, leave the boat immediately. Seek professional assistance. If there is no decrease in pressure, and all the equipment looks proper, use the stove to burn off any fuel in the hose. It is still best to leave the system's valve shut off until the system is professionally checked for possible deterioration and any safety upgrades installed. The main valve must always be shut off when the propane is not in use.

Steering systems

If the boat is equipped with a tiller, usually all connections are visible even while the boat is in the water. A tiller is usually hinged, so that the tiller can swing up out of the way. Inspect all connections for cracks in the metal or the hull and for loose parts.

The wheel steering systems tend to be a complexity of drive wires and fittings. Some manufacturers recommend a particular frequency of lubrication. As always with these wires, check for any fraying, and check for any corrosion on fittings. Any wire with the slightest sign of fraying should be replaced at the first opportunity. Corrosion may just be on the surface and can be cleaned off, but be sure it isn't deep or hiding a crack.

Electrical systems

Sailors can be tinkerers. Your electrical system may have been modified by someone inexperienced. Older boats, like older houses, may not be up to code. A complete description of bringing your electrical system up to code is beyond the scope of this book. Have it checked professionally if you are not familiar with these systems.

The shore power or 110-volt system is particularly dangerous on a boat. Grounding problems and stray current issues can be dangerous. Even a small electrical leak over time can cause major damage through electrolysis. To help protect your boat, *sacrificial zincs* (which aren't always made of zinc) are used, so they will give up their metal, instead of some more critical metal like bolts, shafts, and engine lower units.

Safe sailing is fun sailing. Do everything you can think of to keep your boat, and yourself, safe.

HIGH WAVES, STRONG WINDS, AND SAFE SAILING IN ALL CONDITIONS

> *"To reach a port, we must set sail—*
> *Sail, not tie at anchor—*
> *Sail, not drift."*
>
> FRANKLIN D. ROOSEVELT

THE NINETEENTH STEP: PREDICTING SAILING CONDITIONS AND ANTICIPATING WEATHER-RELATED PROBLEMS

The mass media's weather forecasts cannot be relied upon to provide timely and pertinent information to the sailor.

Weather

Before, and during, your sail, use many sources of weather information. Over time, or over distance, the weather you experience can change. Your eyes and skin are the best, most up-to-date source of current weather information.

Sometimes the weather will change before any forecaster can issue a warning. Be wary of changes in the general type and shape of clouds. Take particular note of the various forms of mid-level clouds called cumulus. There are fair-weather as well as storm cumulus clouds, which look different. Be wary of any clouds rapidly forming or becoming taller. The most dangerous thunderstorms are accompanied by clouds with anvil-shaped tops. The point of the anvil is often pointed in the direction of the storm's travel. Stay clear. Winds can rapidly shift and increase in velocity near storms, and lightning can travel great distances. A shift in wind direction accompanied by a change in temperature may indicate an approaching front, or just be the difference in temperature between wind from shore and wind coming over a long stretch of water. The clouds can be your earliest tip-off.

Numerous photos of storm clouds can be seen on the Internet, in various forms and from various angles. Learn to recognize them. Assume these clouds are bringing strong gusts with them. Usually the gusts are coming generally from the direction these clouds are moving. The gust may arrive well before these clouds are overhead. Always watch for gusts. These can be seen in advance of their arrival by their effect upon the water. Gusts form

Figure 5.1. The darker areas with small waves are the areas with the strongest winds. There is also often a bright area from the sun going past the cloud's edge.

rough water. On otherwise calmer waters, gusts will cause dark spots on the water. The gusts may not have time to build large waves but will make the water darker, as the developing wavelets will be less reflective than a still pool. The technique of spotting areas of stronger and weaker winds by their effect upon the water is useful also for avoiding areas of calm winds and spotting the relatively stronger patches. This can make for a successful sailing day when winds are spotty and weak, or let you win a race.

Learn to "read" wind speed and direction from flags, the movement of trees, and the development of waves and wavelets. A valid assumption is that to get away from the blanketing effects of trees and buildings along the shore, one must typically sail a distance of at least seven times the height of these. Also, assume the winds are stronger aloft than they are on deck. The water has some friction on the wind, slowing it more the closer to the water one gets. The wind can be noticeably stronger on the upper third of your sail than the lower portion. This can necessitate having the upper part of the sails twist, so that both the lower portion and the upper portion are aligned with the wind direction. Buddy Melges, as an inshore racer, had particular need to read the winds near shore on small lakes. Among the tricks he said he used was to watch cows, which tend to face away from the direction of the wind.

You are already familiar with various broadcast and Internet sources of weather information. Check the weather radar, and check more than one forecast service. Add to these a source that provides wave height, tidal, and current wind-speed information.

NOAA has a wonderful, free Internet site giving wind speed, wave height, and current forecast for the major navigable bodies of water. Click on *play* and it will take you forward through several days of forecast. Weather buoys now have their own websites, showing information on wave height, frequency, and direction; wind/gust speed and direction; currents; water temperature; and more. Don't leave home without obtaining that information.

As mentioned, have access at all times to a weather forecast, such as NOAA weather radio. It is inevitable that at some time you will get caught in weather worse than anticipated. The weather can change very quickly. Note also that the weather, and especially the waves, at the harbor or beach may be much different from that on the open waters.

If you leave a harbor that is sheltered from the wind, and the harbor you head to is exposed to the wind, the waves will be quite a bit larger at your destination. The waves will be behind you, and your boat will accelerate as you surf down them. If the waves catch you at an angle, they will try to turn your boat. It will be difficult to slow your boat down with the wind behind you. Anticipate this! Your first lesson in preparing for heavy weather is to simulate large waves behind you. Passing powerboats will oblige, if their behavior is boorish. See how your boat wants to turn depending on the angle of the wave to the boat. See how the boat's speed increases and decreases along the wave. Racers learn to increase speed by surfing their boats on the larger waves; the waves do more than rock the boat.

If you are caught in larger waves, you will be limited in the directions you can travel comfortably. If you have the option, try steering so the bow is just a slight angle from approaching the waves straight on. Keep the boat moving, so that you can keep steering. Steer to avoid the worst parts of the waves.

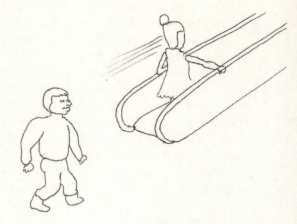

imagine a group of people trying to walk
the *wrong way* on a moving walkway

Figure 5.2. Contrary current. (Drawing by Clare Rosean)

The most dangerous waves are breakers, like the ones you've seen along the beach. Waves break when they reach shallower water. Even water twice as deep as the wave heights can cause waves to break. A regular wave is just a rise and fall of water. A breaking wave has a rolling effect on a boat. Never, ever, allow your boat to turn sideways to a breaking wave. Face into all waves that may break or are breaking, or face away from them. Avoid them entirely if at all possible. Remember that the water under breaking waves is shallower. If the chart shows seven feet of water depth, even if that is accurate, your five-foot-draft boat will hit the bottom hard in four-foot waves. If you see breakers, even if they don't look large enough to be dangerous themselves, the shallower water they are breaking in is very dangerous. Assume there is a rock, reef, or submerged island, and avoid it entirely.

Current-enhanced waves

When a current goes the opposite direction of the wind, wave-building is out of proportion to the wind speed and even to the wind speed combined with the speed of the current. This is because the current bunches up the waves, making them much steeper and higher than they were before they encountered the current. This is why the Gulf Stream, and many harbor entrances, can frequently be very rough in modest winds. The waves pile more closely together like people bunching up as they head toward a moving walkway going the wrong way, or get spread out like people entering a moving walkway going in their direction (see Figure 5.2).

If you are sailing in a current, and either the wind shifts or the current shifts with the tide, the waves will change. At harbor entrances in particular, tides or river currents can raise large waves. These can also cause sand bars to form. The large waves will break at the shallower sand bar. This can become an impassible barrier.

Sailing in sudden storms

This chapter is for emergency use only. It is not complete enough to recommend it as a sole source for planned trips that risk heavy-weather sailing. It is for the unexpected storm.

If you are caught in a thunderstorm, assume there will be strong wind gusts, increased waves, and electrical activity.

Everyone aboard must wear a life jacket. Everyone on deck must be tethered to the boat.

If it is an electrical storm, stay away from all metal. This isn't completely possible; there is always some metal nearby. Stay away in particular from the mast and its supporting wires and chainplates. If shipping is nearby or likely, be sure to keep a careful watch out, especially if you have no propulsion. If you are steering, put only one hand on the tiller and the other in your lap to reduce your exposure to lightning strikes.

Prepare your boat for strong winds and seas. Often the very first gust of wind is one of the strongest. You should be able to see it coming in daylight, but it is far more difficult to spot at night; look for a darker, rougher patch of water or for dirt carried by the wind. Reduce sail area before the gust hits. You may want to take all sails down and motor. Secure all lowered sails and loose equipment. However, the churning waters can make your engine fail (often this is because of sediment in the fuel tank getting stirred up and clogging the filters) as we discussed in Day Four. Accordingly, reducing sail to a reefed main alone makes a lot of sense. Later, more sail area can be added if you feel comfortable. Prevent water from entering. Secure all hatches, ports, and *washboards*. Be sure the cockpit drains are clear. Close off the *companionway* hatch or door. Secure any cockpit stowage, especially a *lazarette* hatch that could spill water into the cabin. Have the bilge pump ready: the intake hose led to a proper spot; the output hose over the side. If the cockpit drains clog, try blowing them out with your compressed air horn to clear them quickly. Use a wet rag along the edge of the horn to help seal the air so it flows into the drain.

Thus secured, your boat will not sink and will not capsize, provided there are no extremely large breaking waves. If there are, you must keep your bow towards them. You can choose to outlast the storm like that. So, while the nearest harbor may be your best choice, consider how difficult the entrance will be under conditions that will worsen as the winds increase. If the harbor is unfamiliar, it is

AIR HORN

To clear a cockpit drain quickly, use a blast of the air horn into the drain. This will clear cobwebs and leaves but not structural problems. As soon as possible after blasting, check the drain hoses for leaks into the boat.

your business to determine if it is safer to risk entry to it. This is one reason you should study the chart of any harbor near your route.

The regular rise and fall of waves will slow you down as you climb them and speed you up as you descend. As you climb the wave, it is essential to maintain enough speed to steer. Otherwise, you are helpless as the wave steepens in front of you. It is also essential to control your descent when going down the wave. Be sure to turn your bow a bit away from the bottom of the wave, so that you do not hit the next rising wave too directly straight on. This can slow you down suddenly, just when you need to maintain speed. Worse, it can submerge your bow.

When planning for long-duration voyages, where storms are likely, consider the use of different types of *sea anchors*, trailing lines, a storm trysail or fourth reef in the mainsail, a satellite phone, a raft, and many other items beyond this book's scope. There are forecasters who, for a fee, will provide suggested departure *weather windows* and routing advice. Select a source based upon his qualifications and the recommendations of fellow travelers. Most will keep you updated of any changes in the forecasts, but you need to have the radio gear set up to receive such messages. This usually entails a single sideband radio and antenna, a modem, a computer and related gear, or a satellite phone.

Sailing in fog

Someday, you may find your navigation gear gives out in the fog. Just from being observant and developing and keeping good habits, you will find your way home (hopefully *Today!*).

Your GPS will lead you home, but make sure it is not leading you to an obstruction, a special danger in fog. If you have no electronics, set a compass course for your destination. As always, double check your charts for obstructions from your current location to the destination. This may be different from your planned voyage; you may opt to head directly to an alternate harbor. There are a number of electronic safety aids useful in good visibility that are even more useful in fog. These are radar and AIS (automatic identification systems) and radar reflectors.

Listen carefully for sounds of other foghorns, engines, conversations from other boats, and, especially, breaking waves.

You should sound your foghorn. When under sail, the proper signal is one long blast, followed immediately with two short every two minutes. Under power, sound one long blast every minute. An occasional "securité" call informing others of your speed and direction would not hurt. Marine radio operation was summarized in Day Three, the seventeenth step.

You can find your way home in the fog with your GPS out of action. Estimate your initial location and keep track of your speed and heading to update your estimated position. Use your depth sounder. The charts can have drawn on them *contour lines*. These connect places of equal depth. Pick an appropriate contour line to follow home; even better, pick a low one and a high one to stay between. Use your ears, too. Look in your chart for fog horns or bells, on lighthouses or buoys, to help you find your way.

Sailing at night

You will eventually become comfortable with sailing at night. The winds can be more steady. Sunburn is an impossibility. Your cruising range is increased. Your first trip at night should just be a local cruise, returning to your original, familiar harbor. As you leave your harbor in the nighttime, take a good look at it several times as you depart. Get familiar with how to safely return to it in the reduced visibility of nighttime.

The principle new skill you must learn, over time, is the meaning of lights. Each time you see a navigation light, learn what it means. Start with these concepts. If you see a ship's light, and it is red, that means that light is on the port, or left, side of the ship. You do not have right-of-way. Think of the red light as a stoplight. You may continue to travel but not in a direction that gets in the other boat's way. If you see a green light, you are the privileged vessel, but be cautious in crossing her. It is always safer to pass astern of the other ship. Assume the other boat hasn't spotted you, and act accordingly.

Each time you see a set of navigation lights on another vessel, learn what they indicate. Each class of vessel, by size and type, has distinctive lights. Always stay out of their way. If you see both a red and a green light on the same ship, its bow is pointing toward you. You might not be able to tell if it is stopped, accelerating, or decelerating.

Shoreline lights are generally simpler. Lighthouses have a distinctive lighting pattern, which is indicated on your charts. The rule "red right returning" applies to channel and harbor entrance lights. Only some obstructions and hazards are lit.

Pick the right night to start with. Ease into night sailing by picking a night with a good weather forecast and plenty of moonlight. Be sure to dress warmly. It often seems colder on the water at night. Make sure you have all your navigation lights on and properly operating. Assume your lights nonetheless will fail. Take a couple of flashlights. If the lights fail, shine your flashlight on the sails. Feel free to get attention by shining the light toward another vessel if you feel in danger.

Let your eyes adjust to the darkness. It takes about 30 minutes for one's eyes to fully adjust to darkness and only seconds to lose their darkness adaptation. Even dim red lights can reduce darkness adaptation. Opening a computer screen, lighting a match, or using a lighter will mean that for many minutes you are blinded by the darkness. Before any light is turned on, close one eye. That eye will remain dark-adapted. Tell your crew to let you know before turning on any light or opening the cabin door.

Sailing after dark requires knowing from your charts what to avoid. You can no longer rely on eyeball navigation. Breakwalls and other hazards obvious in daylight can be surprisingly difficult to see after sunset. Some important channel markers are unlit. Night time sailing can be safe, if the skipper stays alert, keeps his eyes adapted, knows where he is and that he is nowhere near a dangerous shoal, etc. One distinct rule: never enter an unfamiliar harbor at night.

It is more difficult to spot a change in the weather. Reducing sail area as a preventative measure just before nightfall has much to commend it.

Your telltales, and the wind vane, will be very difficult to see without lighting. You may need to go forward to adjust the sails or some other chore. It is all the more critical, for safety, to keep yourself and any crew on deck, especially forward, tethered to the boat and wearing a PFD. In your pockets should be a waterproof flashlight and whistle. A throwable cushion should have a waterproof light stick such as a Cyalume™ attached.

Figure 5.4. "Savannah's Reflections" (Courtesy Katie Colgan's Studio)

Because you will have trouble seeing waves, you may get splashed. Wear or have available a waterproof jacket for the coldest temperatures possible.

Your home harbor will look especially beautiful when you return after sunset.

# *NAVIGATION*

> *"It is not the ship so much as the skillful sailing that assures the [successful] sailing."*
>
> GEORGE WILLIAM CURTIS

THE TWENTIETH STEP: FIND YOUR WAY

Navigation should never be just by eyes and GPS.

Your navigation tools

A *navigation kit* consists of:

- Printed charts of your home harbor, your destination harbor, all alternate harbors, and the waters in between
- Artist pencils (these are thicker than regular pencils and won't cut the chart)
- A mounted compass and a hand-bearing compass
- A dimmed red light
- A course plotter (parallel ruler or protractor)
- Dividers (drafting compass)
- A calculator (for time and speed)
- A depth sounder
- A knotmeter
- A GPS

A convenient addition to the preceding is a chartplotter, or a cell phone, computer, or tablet with navigation software.

Navigation in general

Not all forms of navigation are equal. Your preferred hierarchy of navigation aids is:

1. Charts and compass. This allows you to easily and safely note shallows and other dangers the GPS might not adequately display.
2. Visual aids. Your chart and compass work hand in hand with these.
3. Dead reckoning. This is the practice of estimating your position from observing course and speed, and time and distance from various points along the way.
4. GPS. This includes various apps for Android, iPhone, iPad, tablets, and other devices. If you are using electronics not designed for marine use, enclose them in a waterproof, not merely splash-proof, container.

Download or purchase your local charts. You can obtain the charts of your area on the Internet: http://www.nauticalcharts.noaa.gov. The price is the same as the price of sailboat fuel. Yay! It's free.

Learn the meaning of every notation on the chart of your area. The meaning of every notation is found in a document called Chart No. 1, also found in www.nauticalcharts.noaa.gov. I recommend you buy it. It is a lengthy document and difficult to search through on the computer. It is much easier to just open the book with the charts in front of you, so you can look up the meaning of each notation.

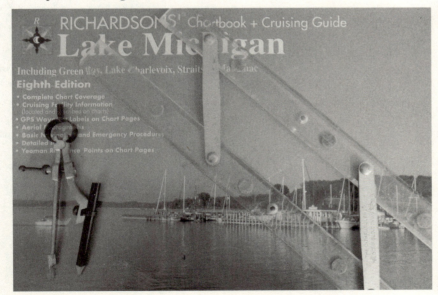

Figure 6.1.

Start with the most detailed chart that includes your local harbor. Also obtain the charts that cover at the greatest available detail your entire intended sailing area and especially any harbor you may want to enter in an emergency. Although many now rely on their on-board computer, I urge you to print out all the important charts. Despite having a dedicated navigator and some of the finest electronic navigation equipment in existence, a multi-million-dollar Volvo ocean racer ran into a reef and was virtually destroyed. The reason was the failure to use paper charts costing at most a few dollars.

Note on the top left of U.S. charts how depth is marked. Depth markings, known as *soundings* will be stated in feet or fathoms. Note that the soundings are to mean low water, which on inland lakes refers to an average dry spell, and on the ocean and tidal waters refers to an average low tide. Those and possible errors in your depth sounder will affect your readings. Nonetheless, when you know your actual depth and convert the depth shown on the chart to the water level at that time, it will show you the contour line you are on. That, plus your time and speed formula, will give you a line of position. If the estimated line of position intersects a depth contour sharply, you know your approximate position.

With the chart out, overlay a chart of the currents in that area. We will classify currents as tide-driven, river-driven, and wind-driven. There are also geological currents such as the Gulf Stream. If you are on a lake, you may still encounter currents of the less predictable, wind-driven variety or the flow of a river into the lake.

Tides are predictable because the gravitational pull of the sun and the moon causes them. When the sun, moon, and earth are all in a line, the pull of the sun and the moon on the oceans is strongest. When the sun, moon, and earth form a right angle, the tides are the weakest (see Figure 6.2). Because the moon is

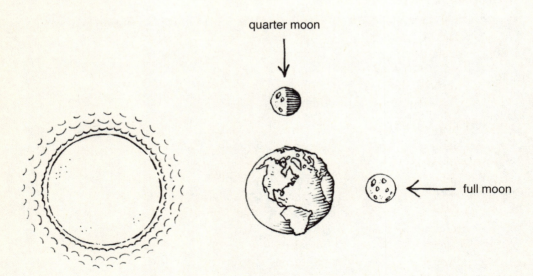

Figure 6.2. (Drawing by Christopher Hoyt)

circling the earth every 29½ days, each day the maximum and minimum tides occur about 50 minutes later than the day before. If the moon is moving toward first or last quarter, it is moving further from the earth-sun line, and the tides will be diminishing. If the moon is moving toward full or new, it is moving closer to the earth-sun line, and the tides will be larger the next day but arriving, as always, about 50 minutes later.

The tide-driven currents can therefore be predicted long in advance with great accuracy. They reach a maximum and minimum either once or twice a day dependent on your location; the tide-driven current speed drops to zero at each high and low tide; the tide-driven current is at a maximum midway between the times of the high and the low tide and reverses direction at each high and low; water flows in from the ocean, raising the water level as the tide flows in (floods) and lowering it as the tide flows out (ebbs). Tide times and heights are tremendously influenced by geography, but in a generally predictable manner. Topography's effects on tides include the distance along the channel or bay to the open ocean and the shape of the waters—a bay with a wide entrance and narrowing, shoaling channel can have huge tides.

The tides will carry far into rivers that spill into the ocean. Tides along the East Coast of the United States can be substantial and generally have two roughly equal highs and lows daily. Along the West Coast, the two highs and two lows are usually not equal, with one pair being more extreme than the other.

You need to know tides along coastal areas because:

1. They can deprive you of sufficient water beneath your keel.
2. They can deprive you of sufficient clearance beneath bridges and wires.
3. They can impede your progress or rush you along.
4. A tide running against the wind will result in steeper waves.

Your tide calculations begin with a tide table or tide calculator telling you the principal times of high and low tide and the principal water level change at the nearby open shore.

Next, obtain and examine the local tide chart. It will give you the *offsets*, the time difference between high tide at the open shore and high tide locally, which will depend generally on how far into a bay you are, and hence how long it will take the shoreline high tide to reach you. It will also show maximum currents, sometimes with great specificity. From these figures you can calculate when you will have a favorable current, when the current will turn against you, and, should you need a high tide or no (*slack*) current, when you must arrive.

As you do this, make sure that you have sufficient clearance under your keel along your path, as well as above the mast at any and all bridges and wires. Bridge clearances are stated for mean high water, but some tides are higher than mean, and wave action can raise your mast still higher. Similarly, the water depths are listed for mean low water, but some tides are lower than the mean low. Not only can waves deny your keel even the lesser depth, but tidal areas and areas with waves will cause sandy or muddy bottoms to flow a bit, forming shallows that may not be accounted for in the charts or even the updates. Allow for extra clearance. Conversely, you may use high tides to cross a shallows and low tides when necessary to clear a bridge that would otherwise be just a bit too low.

Your local boat shop or marina should have your local tide information. It is also available on the Internet, covering your area. Tidal information on the Internet can be found at http://tidesite.appspot.com/. Pick your harbor; it will give details. NOAA's official tidal information is available at http://tidesandcurrents.noaa.gov/tide_predictions.shtm. Be sure you are using the correct time in interpreting any tide table. The tide table could be in Standard Time, while your watch shows Daylight Saving. Or, the table could be in Universal Time. Also, tide tables are published annually; last year's would be useless.

The tide tables show the heights of the low and high tides, as well as their timing. But you are in a sailboat, and the time of your arrival is going to be a bit questionable. Refer to the Rule of Twelfths (Figure 6.3). Verify the time

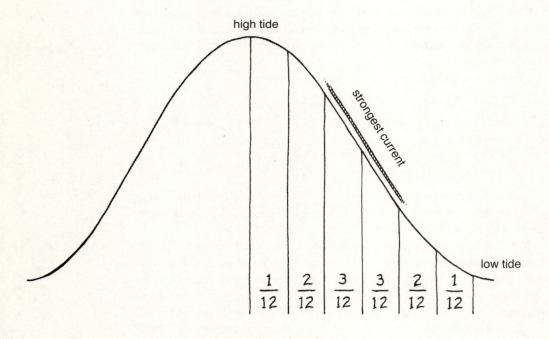

Figure 6.3. (Drawing by Christopher Hoyt)

between high and low tides. The Rule of Twelfths describes the approximate rate of rise or fall of the tides. The tide's rise and fall is not linear; it speeds and slows in a predictable manner. The tide's rise and fall will be $1/12^{th}$ of the total distance in the first one-sixth of the time, $2/12^{ths}$ in the next sixth, $3/12^{ths}$ in the next sixth, another $3/12^{ths}$ in the next sixth, $2/12^{ths}$ in the next sixth, and $1/12^{th}$ in the last sixth. Let's apply this. Say we find we arrive after high tide in an area where the tides are twice daily. There is a six-hour period between high and low tide. Say the tide range is 12 feet. This means if we arrive one hour after high tide, the tide is now lower by one foot. If another hour later, the tide is lowered by another two feet. The total in the two hours is three feet, meaning the tide is now nine feet. In the next hour, the tide will drop three feet, for a tide of six feet above the low. In the fourth hour, the tide will drop three more feet and is now three feet above the low. In the next hour, the tide drops two feet, and it reaches the low in another hour, dropping only one foot. If we missed our window of opportunity, we have to wait for the tide to rise. When it does, the tidal current will reverse and may send us to or away from the shallows and may speed or slow us toward our destination. Remember, the currents will be strongest when the water is rising or falling rapidly.

River currents are consistent through the day and fairly consistent over a period of days, but they are affected by rainfall upriver in the river basin. They travel in one direction only, except where the tide overwhelms the current. The friction of the river bank and bottom can slow the currents. On a bend in the river, the current is often stronger on the outside than the inside of the curve.

Wind-driven currents can form over a large body of water dependent, of course, on wind speed and the duration of the wind in a given direction. NOAA will do its best to forecast this. A wind-driven current approaching a bay can turn in unanticipated directions. An example of this is the passage between Green Bay and Lake Michigan. In the age of sail, with cargo ships unable to sail upwind, this area was given the name of Death's Door. The local chamber of commerce prefers the name Door County, which became fabulous sailing territory with the upwind ability of the modern yacht.

Begin to visualize what the chart means in the real world

Your first homework assignment in navigation is to compare the real-world features in photos or satellite imagery with the chart's representation of those same features. Over time, you will learn to visualize the features you see on the chart. Planning and plotting your route should be done at home or at the dock, not under way.

Figure 6.4. (Photo courtesy Dan Waters)

Visualize the harbor entrance: where it is, how you enter, which way and how far, and where you must turn to stay in the channel (the safe and proper lane of travel in the harbor).

Hazards may be marked with a floating navigation aid, which can include a bell or light, or may include a marker only visible during the day, or may be completely unmarked. If marked, the hazard's marking may be shrouded in fog, the bell may not be ringing (bell buoys are rung by the action of waves; if waves are absent, so is the sound). Lights may be inoperative. "Red right returning" is valuable as far as it goes, but sometimes the returning direction may be ambiguous. Red buoys have a different shape than green buoys. Docks and other objects may intrude into an otherwise direct path from point *a* to *b*; these may be noted on the charts. Some features may be too new to be included. Shallow spots and sandbars can move. Water levels can change, so a shallow spot may allow passage at some times and not others. Do not assume the chart is absolutely accurate. Inaccuracies

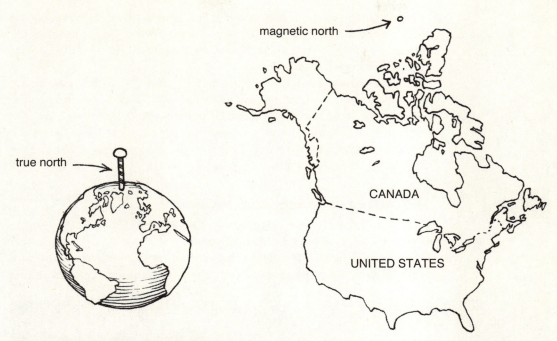

Figure 6.5. (**Drawing by Christopher Hoyt**)

from various causes creep into charts. In one incident, a family whose intended course was perhaps a dozen miles from a reef struck it. It is uncertain if the cause was a chart error or a navigation error, because the charts sank with the boat. While their accuracy is not 100 percent, it is far better to rely on a combination of charts and caution than blind luck.

The compass rose, true north, and magnetic north

Find the compass rose. There may be several located on a chart, especially one covering a wide area. Always use the one closest to your course. Note that there are two circles in the compass rose. The outer circle is in *degrees true*, from which your actual heading is derived. The inner circle is in *degrees magnetic*. The North

Figure 6.6.

Pole, at the top of the arctic, is not at the same location as the magnetic north pole, which is in Canada. You will want to write both courses, magnetic and actual, on your chart. Know whether your GPS is set to degrees magnetic or degrees true (see Figure 6.5).

Locations and headings on a paper chart are found with the assistance of parallel rulers, which allow you to "walk" your lines of direction to the compass rose, at least one of which is on every chart.

In Figure 6.6, the navigator is preparing the course at home before the cruise. She is holding the parallel ruler on the course line and has slid the other half of the ruler over the compass rose.

Measuring distances and position

There is a distance graph on the edges of every chart. Dividers are great to measure mileage. A ruler could also be used.

Note in Figure 6.7 the dividers are used by setting them on the distance scale. The compass rose with the routes is visible on the left. The parallel rule

Figure 6.7.

is off to the left. The dividers are placed on the route to measure its distance, or you can use a ruler. Inches of distance can be converted to mileage using the chart's reference, e.g., "one inch equals 3.7 miles."

> *"I am a strong believer in luck, and I find the harder I work, the more I have of it."*
>
> BENJAMIN FRANKLIN

Avoidance of hazards, visible and hidden

The location of most underwater hazards can be gleaned from the chart. What kind of markers, if any, are at these hazards? Does each have a bell, a light, or neither? With reference to your course, is the hazard to the left or right, in front of, or behind the marker? It is vanishingly rare to have all points of a hazard marked in any way, except on the chart itself. You could head 100 feet to one side or the other of the marker and wind up right on the hazard. Enter this data in your log both as a reference and because the act of writing will help you remember. What is the draft of your boat? Will you have enough depth at low tide?

When you leave the harbor, practice comparing your GPS speed, location, and course with your observations. Over time, the accuracy of your estimate of speed, location, and distance will improve. Compare your position with the chart for practice identifying chart notations.

To check your position and note it on the chart, you may take a bearing from two or three objects and run a line on the chart from each bearing you took. You will be near the location those points intersect. If there is only one point you can reference, you can take two bearings from it, a period of time apart. It is best if the bearings are separated by a time that is a simple fraction of an hour, as in 10 minutes, one-sixth of an hour. Run the two bearings on a line from the object. Take your dividers and set them apart by the estimated distance you have covered in that time; then line them up with your direction of travel. You will be near the point where the lines diverge by the distance you have travelled.

Check the *Coast Pilot* for your area. This will have updates for your chart. Essentially, it tells you some places, but not all, where your chart is wrong. It is also at www.nauticalcharts.noaa.gov. Check also the *Local Notice to Mariners* for additional updates.

When navigating by compass, know the error in your compass. When the compass indicates 45 degrees (northeast), your actual heading may differ because of metal, magnetic, and electrical influences.

To calibrate your compass properly, head out into an open space far from any magnetic influences. Empty your pockets, and take off any metal belt buckles, etc. Place these far from the compass. Note which ordinary navigation gear is on: lights, radar, and especially your stereo can affect the compass. Now, line up a *pelorus*, a device through which you can sight angles with the centerline of your boat. Determine your heading, continuing in 15- or 30-degree iterations; this is best done starting from true north, 0 or 360 degrees. Call out your heading, and have your assistant write down the true heading and the compass heading. Use your compass rose to write on the same log the local difference between true north and magnetic north. Keep this variation chart by your compass as you navigate. If later you travel to a location with a different magnetic/true north differential, you will need to make the appropriate correction.

Learn to recognize and avoid hazards to others. For example, scuba divers use a distinctive flag that marks only their approximate location. A diver could surface a good distance from the flag.

Learn the visual aids to navigation. There can be differences internationally, but in the United States, there are four principal mnemonics to remember:

1. "Red right returning." The red-colored buoys, lights, or *daymarks* (see below) are positioned so that you leave them to the boat's right-hand, or starboard, side when returning to the harbor. The green ones are to be on your left side. Leaving the harbor, it is the opposite.

2. TERN (like the sea bird). *T*riangle, *E*ven numbered, *R*ed, and *N*un. The so-called daymarks, which are equivalent to the red ones in "red right returning," are shaped like a triangle. The red ones have even numbers. The nun shape is a shape specific to the red buoys, resembling, it is said, a nun's head covering (not really; it is a kind of truncated cone at the top).

3. COGS (like cogs in a wheel). *C*an, *O*dd numbers, *G*reen, and *S*quare. The buoys are green, shaped like a large tin can, and have odd numbers, and the day markers are green squares.

4. "Red port wine." Red lights are on the port (left) side of all boats. This, you will note, would equate to "red left leaving."

Photos of each type of navigation marker (buoy) can be found on the Internet. You will also find some markers that are striped green and red. These generally indicate the center of a channel. Stay to the right of the center of the channel. Treat it like the center stripe of a road. Watch also for preferred courses for commercial shipping. These shipping lanes should be crossed at right angles as quickly as possible, keeping a sharp lookout. If your cruising ground is near such a shipping lane, an AIS (automatic identification system) is especially recommended.

Overreliance on charting GPS units is dangerous. It is too easy to overlook important features as one scans the route on the electronic chart. Be sure the data entered into the GPS is correct. When entering a data point, make sure you are using the proper format. It could be entered as degrees, minutes and seconds, or it could be degrees, minutes, and hundredths of minutes. Your location could be one-third of a mile off by using the wrong format. That is enough to cause a collision or grounding. Be sure the GPS is set properly to interpret the charts loaded into it. A downloaded chart has a certain center of reference, which you can think of as the distance from one corner of the chart to a point of reference on the earth. If the GPS isn't set to the same format as the chart, errors must occur.

Dead reckoning

Dead reckoning refers to a deducted, reasoned estimate of position. Remember the rule: the prudent navigator never relies on only one form of navigation. Dead reckoning is your backup method. It is always available. It requires no electronics. It should always be used and verified with visual references. The formula for speed, time, and distance can be remembered visually:

$$\frac{\text{Distance}}{\text{Speed} \times \text{Time}}$$

If you know two of the factors, the third gets calculated. Distance divided by speed equals time. Speed times time equals distance. Distance divided by time equals speed.

Mark off your estimated positions on your paper chart every hour. Your chart will show some distinctive features on shore or marks anchored in the water. Use those to corroborate your line of position. Suppose you see a buoy a mile or so from your line of position. Carefully measure the distance along your route to the point you are nearest the buoy (it will be perpendicular to your route when you are nearest it). Calculate the time of closest approach, and watch for it with your binoculars. Use your hand-bearing compass to verify when it is 90 degrees from your course. Estimate its distance. You have now confirmed your navigation. Adjust your course as necessary.

Once you have determined a safe course, the next skill is keeping the boat on that course. You have several means to do so:

1. Stationary objects. If there are stationary objects ahead, look at those. Be sure you are sighting straight ahead in line with the boat. If you are to the side of the boat, as common in sailing, sighting straight along the bow will mean you will be looking at an angle to the boat's direction of travel.

2. GPS. This is too delayed, even with a top unit, to tell you when you are not heading straight. It can take several seconds to respond to a change in direction, so you will not be able to steer a straight course by GPS alone.

3. Compass. The compass responds very promptly to a change in heading. It takes some practice to get used to steering to a compass heading. If you turn right, the numbers will increase; they will decrease when turning left. There is also a sudden jump at north, 360 and 0 degrees. Remember that a hand-held compass will be affected by any metal nearby, in your boat, or your pockets. Its accuracy will change depending on who holds it and where it is.

Figure 6.8. Numbers rise to the right and lower to the left. (Drawing by Clare Rosean)

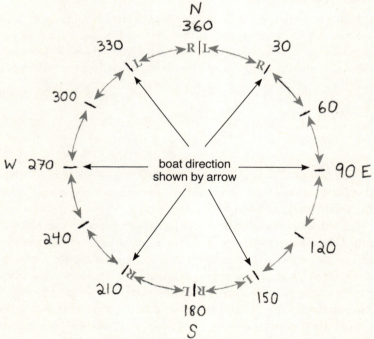

Regardless of boat directions, numbers rise
to the right and lower to the left

Always be aware of the location of obstructions and hazards. You will be travelling in at least a slightly different direction than you are pointed at because of the effect of waves, currents, winds, and the boat's *leeway* (its built-in failure to hold a straight course). Therefore, even if the obstructions are not on your exact path, you should still be aware of all and be ready to avoid them in case your actual position differs from your expected position.

What to do if you run aground or get caught on ropes

You can run aground on a shallow spot or have a related problem by getting caught in an underwater object, such as the lobster pots on the U.S. northeast coast. Handled properly, and with a little luck, it will be a mere inconvenience.

If you run aground, make certain the boat isn't holed, or taking on water. Then, assure no further damage is caused to the boat. This usually means making sure you do not get blown or driven by the winds further onto the obstruction.

In the smaller boats, get free by raising the centerboard and rudder enough to float off. If safe, you could tether or tie yourself to the boat, then step out of the boat onto the sea or lake floor and push. If strong currents or dangerous sea life prevent you from getting off, you must use the more complicated procedures for large boats.

LARGER BOATS. If the tide is rising, merely setting an anchor positioned so that your boat maintains its location will allow it to rise off the bottom. If there is a falling tide, you may have little time to act. If there is a chance the hull will actually end up on its side, be prepared to set cushions under the endangered side of the boat, and try to get the boat, if it must fall to the side, to fall to the safest direction.

With water levels steady, you have time to plan a course of action. Look all around the boat. Determine in which direction the boat has the deepest water. A line with a weight can be used to determine this. Then, with the boat prevented from being driven further aground, raise the keel. This is done by tilting the boat. However, if you have a winged keel, this may cause one wing or the other to dig in. To tilt the boat, ease the boom out to the best side to tilt the boat and put a lot of weight on it—all it can stand.

Another procedure is called *kedging*. The anchor is taken in a dinghy in the direction of your best exit from the obstruction, as far as possible, and set properly in the best holding ground. The anchor rode can be attached to a halyard (causing the boat to tilt more) or directly to the best positioned, most powerful winch, and the boat is literally winched off the obstruction. As this is done, care must be taken not to damage the boat; the rudder and hull may be far more vulnerable than the keel.

If you need a tow, call for one on channel 16. This should not be a life-threatening situation, so Mayday should not be used. When the tow arrives, get confirmation this is a tow, not a salvage (which is far, far more expensive). Once the tow line is secure, return to the helm to steer the boat in the direction of travel. It would also be good to agree on a radio channel for both vessels to monitor in case something goes haywire.

If the boat should get caught on a rope, immediately put the gearshift in neutral and shut off the engine. Do not attempt to use the engine to work your way out. Severe prop, shaft, and even engine damage may result. Try to find the line with a boat hook, and pull the line as far forward to the bow of the boat as possible. The

Figure 6.9.

line may disengage in that process. Hopefully, no one will have to dive into the water to clear it with a knife. That is a last resort.

Sail to another harbor

Transcript of a radio conversation released on October 10, 1998, by the chief of British naval operations between a British and an Irish radio operator, off the Irish coast:

> Irish: "Please divert your course 15 degrees south to avoid a collision."
>
> British: "Recommend you divert your course 15 degrees north to avoid a collision."

> Irish: "Negative. You will have to divert your course 15 degrees south to avoid a collision."
>
> British: "This is the captain of a British naval ship. I say again, divert YOUR course."
>
> Irish: "I say again, you will have to divert YOUR course."
>
> British: "This is the captain of the HMS *Brittania*! The second largest ship in the British Atlantic fleet. We are accompanied by three cruisers, three destroyers, and numerous support vessels. I demand you change your course 15 degrees north;

Figure 6.10. The Norwegian tall ship *Sorlandet* returns to Chicago.

I say again, that is 15 degrees north, or counter-measures will be undertaken to ensure the safety of this ship."
Irish: "We are a lighthouse. Your call."

Once principles of navigation are learned, a trip to another harbor can be planned. Proper navigation is one of the keys to safe sailing. While the oft-repeated story of the British fleet threatening a lighthouse is false, on April 28, 1983, the *Enterprise*, one of the greatest nuclear-powered ships ever built, ran aground on a well-charted shallows. She was stuck on Bishops Rock on the Cortes Bank near San Francisco for hours and had to be pulled off by tugboats on a rising tide. The lesson to be learned, as the *Enterprise* and the *Titanic* learned the hard way, is do not let overconfidence overcome your need to be vigilant against avoidable hazards.

Following are the steps to take as you prepare to sail to another harbor. Plan a safe route. Use paper charts to determine your safe route. Spend some time looking at the local charts in the comfort of your house. Note the location of each harbor that you might choose to stop in, whether for fun or in an emergency. This is both useful in its own right and a drill for learning to use charts. Accurately determine the latitude and longitude of the entrance of each harbor. Write these on the chart. Plan your *waypoints*. Waypoints are the turning points on your voyage. If the harbor has a breakwater (as most do), do not use a waypoint inside the break wall. Heading straight to the waypoint could cause you to hit the wall. Enter the proper waypoints into your boat, maintenance, and navigation logbooks and as waypoints in your GPS. Your GPS will be used to back up or confirm your navigation. Write hazards in the log, noting their locations and noting therefore which headings from which harbors are dangerous, and which are safe, e.g., "to waypoint 37, Bailey's Harbor, headings 33 degrees to 72 degrees are safe, 75 to 95 are no-go, head to waypoint 36 bell R-2 instead. Headings 100 to 180 are safe." I am not aware of a GPS that is designed to incorporate this.

Set directions that allow a sufficient safety zone to assure avoiding any shallows or obstructions. This may involve turns at several places well away from hazards. Draw the lines on the chart using the artist's pencil. Use dividers (a circle scribe from a hardware store is a good substitute), measuring from the chart's scale along the border of the chart. Write down the distance from your harbor entrance to the first waypoint. Use parallel rulers to walk the line from the course line you drew on the chart to the compass rose. Learn both the actual and the magnetic headings, which you will determine from the compass rose. Write the actual (A) and magnetic course (M) on the chart or with a grease pencil on the fiberglass bulkhead of your boat. Write the distance as well. Do this from each waypoint to the next, and so on, concluding with the course and distance from the last waypoint to the destination harbor.

Learn the actual magnetic declination, more commonly called *magnetic variation*. This will doubtless have changed since the chart was produced. For greater accuracy than an outdated chart, use the worksheet at http://www.ngdc.noaa.gov/geomag/declination.shtml.

Compare these distances and locations to your best estimate of boat speed. Will you be heading upwind? Factor in tacking, and make sure no tack could take you to a dangerous location. Factor in your leeway. Check the tide tables and charts to determine how tides will affect you; can you time your trip to gain an assist from the tide?

Create a "Plan B" for an alternate harbor. Have charts for all potential alternate harbors.

Study carefully the best detailed chart available of the destination harbor. Note whether your boat can clear any shallows. Will you need a particular state of tide to enter? Plan your departure so you can arrive in daytime at the proper state of the tide. If there are no vertical clearance issues (bridges, for example) and no problems with tidal currents, a rising tide is recommended entering a harbor to lift your boat off if you wind up aground. Note the forecasted wind direction and strength at your destination harbor.

Once you have the proper weather window, calculate the approximate time you will arrive, let someone know your float plan, and go. You are a real sailor now.

7 BUYING AND OWNING A BOAT

> *"A boat, above all other inanimate things, is personified in man's mind."*
>
> JOHN STEINBECK

Your own porch on the water

THE TWENTY-FIRST STEP: BUYING AND EQUIPPING YOUR BOAT

Don't rush. Take your time. Smell the roses.

What to buy and how to equip your boat

This book is *Learn to Sail Today!* In it, you will find advice on buying a relatively inexpensive first boat, a boat you can buy today and not spend 20 years paying for. Lin and Larry Pardey, among the top couples in the cruising world, exemplify their philosophy, "Go small, go simple, go now." They recommend learning on a 14-foot sailboat. I agree. I think I know which one they mean.

A professional inspection is necessary

It would take several books to describe all aspects of maintenance on all the systems in a yacht. Its systems may include engine, transmission, shaft, propeller, electrical, *head* (toilet), plumbing, refrigerator, stove, heating systems, electronics, bilge pumps, fire extinguishers, hull, keel, rudder and steering gear, rig, lines, lightning protection, sails, and more. All must be regularly inspected and maintained. You can hire people to check these and seek advice. You can read any number of excellent books and articles on these subjects.

Before you buy any sailboat, excepting the simplest dinghy, have it surveyed by a competent surveyor, independent of the seller, whose practice concentrates on sailboats. If you must sign a contract before the survey, make the contract conditional upon an acceptable survey. Be present during the survey; you likely will learn a lot. The surveyor may advise you to have a mechanic survey the engine, a rigger survey the rigging, and a sailmaker evaluate the sails. If your investment is large, the expense of the survey will be minimal in comparison.

The inspection is more detailed than in Day Four. Among the things the surveyor will look for is prior damage, especially if poorly repaired; compliance with boat building standards; delamination of the layers of the material forming the hull; internal rot or wetness; and issues with the integrity of the keel, rudder, and steering systems. The chainplates, which connect the shrouds to the hull, are a particular concern.

Annually, obtain a safety inspection by the Coast Guard Auxiliary. This group is experienced in verifying that the boat's equipment is as required and will explain any issues they discover. They never report their findings to the authorities. This is so boaters will unhesitatingly welcome their inspections. If you pass, they will give you an annual sticker, which tends to dissuade boardings by the authorities;

Figure 7.1. Boats come in all shapes and sizes.

it is proof your equipment is up to snuff. They do not perform structural inspections, so it is up to you to take care of that.

But, before you need a surveyor or the Coast Guard Auxiliary inspection, you need a boat.

Is it fun to sail this boat?

I hope in your six days of sailing you enjoyed a performance yacht or dinghy. You will not want any other kind. A good performing yacht costs no more than a slow one. If you want to someday race your boat, your selection is easy. Your best choice is whatever *one-design* boat in a nearby racing fleet has the largest number of boats in the size, price range, and with the accommodations you want. Racing against identical boats will help you improve your sailing skills.

It is very important that your boat handle well. Understand this crucial point: the difference in handling between a good boat and a bad boat is much greater than the difference between a good car and a bad car. The worst-designed car can successfully drive along any road; not so with boats and what the water can dish out. Such factors as dryness; the feel of the steering; ability to go to windward (both pointing and tracking); stability; ability to recover from excessive heeling or even from a knockdown; strength of the hull, keel, rig, and rudder; and the boat's motion in a seaway all vary from boat to boat. These do not show up just at a glance.

Some important factors in sailing performance

The sails are obviously critical to sailing performance. Have them evaluated by a sail maker. Raising and lowering sails can be a chore, which roller furling almost completely eliminates. It also eliminates in most instances one of the most dangerous activities in sailing: going all the way forward to take down a sail as winds and seas increase. Furling jibs are convenient and a necessity for the use of a larger boat by the less athletic crowd. The only negatives are that the sails are given a shape and a heavy rear edge that slightly compromise their effectiveness. They have a higher clew (the attachment point of the sheet to the sail). This allows the angle of the sheet to the sail to remain more constant as the sail is furled. But that takes away from the sail area, particularly from the lower portion of the sail. Also, as the sail is furled, the sail's shape becomes less optimal. The heavy rear edge (leech) is a sunlight blocking cloth. The most efficient sails will be lighter. (All sail materials are damaged by exposure to sunlight, so they should be covered when not in use. The roller-furled sail has the cover attached to the leech so that only the cover material is exposed to light when the sail is rolled up.)

In-mast mainsail furling is a terrific labor saver but more harmful to performance than jib furling. The furling main cannot have horizontal battens. Battens help by supporting added sailcloth and creating a nice airfoil shape, a gentle curve becoming almost straight at the rear. Their absence hinders upwind performance. The mast is made larger so the sail can furl within; that interferes with airflow at the front. So, the front and rear of the sail, the most important parts, are made worse. With the furler jammed, a main so equipped cannot be quickly lowered in an emergency. Complicating this one-sided presentation, vertical battens can be installed at some expense into a sail designed for furling to somewhat compensate for the loss of the horizontal battens.

Other solutions are roller furling on the boom, a fat boom on which the main can rest, or a series of small lines called a *Dutchman* or *lazy jacks*. The Dutchman and lazy jacks and their variations are low tech, simple, and reliable and require no or only minor modifications to the sails and little or no compromise on sail shape and size. The only negatives are some wear from the lines rubbing the sail and the cost of the larger boom and possibly an electric winch, if desired. An electric winch can handle the chore of hoisting the main and perform other duties as well.

REMEMBER ALWAYS: Be careful using any winch, but especially an electrical one. Do not get your fingers or hands caught.

A fixed propeller dragging in the water slows the boat. A folding or feathering propeller can add a lot of speed under sail. Those can cost a few thousand dollars; finding a boat with a folding or feathering prop is a huge plus. Those are not found on outboards, which do not need them, as the outboard is tilted out of the water.

With old boats, there can be age-related slowness. Roughness in the hull, keel, and rudder slow any boat. This can be fixed with filler, sandpaper, and a lot of elbow grease, followed with several coats of paint. You can do something about the age and wear of the sails (although sails are expensive!), but you cannot fix the keel shape or replace the mast without incredible expense.

Boat builders and boat designers have reputations. Find out; be critical; ask a lot of questions of owners of the type of boat you are considering. The comments of owners of competing designs will be very interesting, too. Before you buy your boat, find out everything you can about that model, or at least about a very similar boat by the same designer and manufacturer.

What size of boat should I buy

I am not a minimalist, but I urge that your first boat be the smallest, simplest one that can possibly satisfy you. This is universal starting a new activity: if you take flying lessons, you will start with a small, single-engine airplane, not a 747. It is a mistake to start out on a larger, complicated yacht. The smaller vessels can be much more responsive, allowing you to see clearly the effect of balance and sail trim as you learn and experiment. It is much harder to evaluate the effect of a change in sail trim or balance (not just heeling, but fore and aft trim as well) if it takes time for the change in speed to occur. Tiller steering will let you feel the pressure on the rudder and will easily let you know the direction the rudder is pointing. This is a huge advantage for beginners and anyone wanting to improve their sailing skills.

**Figure 7.2.
(Photo courtesy
UK Sailmakers)**

Daysailers and dinghies are abundant and very light for easy trailering or cartopping. They have smaller *sailplans* and masts for easier mast raising, rigging, and sail handling. They can be very inexpensive. Many can become overnighters by rigging a simple tent formed by the boom. In this configuration, they are called camper-cruisers. That phrase also can refer to boats with a simple cabin containing little more than berths within.

If your boating dreams involve overnight trips for two to four people, there are even some under-20-foot boats that will comfortably berth that many for a weekend trip, although the accommodations are like a fiberglass tent with cushions. In order to get an enclosed head, with few exceptions you generally must have at least 25 feet of boat. A 30-foot racer-cruiser can have six adults on deck for sailing or drinks and conversation, comfort for the same six in the cabin, an enclosed head with a hot shower, and a small galley (kitchen). So those should be your target sizes: 12 to 14 feet as a first boat, for daytime use by yourself, or yourself and a guest; 15 to 22 feet for overnighting in camper-like comfort; and about 25 feet if an enclosed head is essential. Anything larger than a 30-foot boat is not necessary for anything less ambitious than world cruising and is just plain wrong for your first boat. Be sure to get a vessel that will sail well. Your surveyor will be able to estimate how much it will cost to repair or improve your chosen boat. This can be a significant expense, often a third or more of the purchase price.

For a pre-teen child, the 7.5-foot Optimist dinghy is a popular training boat. According to *Practical Sailor*, it is suitable for youths weighing between 65 and 130 pounds, and 80 percent of the winners at the 2012 Olympics learned some of their skills aboard one. Their problem is they are a bit pokey. If you are single or have a family of just two, consider a boardboat of about 12 to 14 feet, such as the very popular Sunfish™. You can store such a boat in your garage or basement and haul it on your cartop. You can set it up in minutes, not pay for moorings or storage, and learn lots about sailing aboard one. As you zip along low to the water, it is more exhilarating than being higher up, secured in a cockpit behind a cabin trunk. The difference in the experience is like the difference between a motorcycle and a sedan. Yet a small boat can be as safe as a large keelboat, whereas a motorcycle cannot be as safe as a sedan.

A Sunfish, its higher performance cousin, the Laser, and others like it are very responsive, so the novice can clearly see, feel, and learn the effect of sail and rudder trim, while the expert can be thrilled with its speed. Both are best in waters that are not frigid. You will get wet on occasion. The Sunfish is a good racing boat with many fleets, and is easy for the beginner. The Laser is a challenging boat, with great speed. Owning one opens up the possibility of a lifetime of racing against some of the finest sailors in the world, without having the race determined by who has the better boat and fatter wallet. However, it is not a beginner's boat with the standard rig. It may be with the optional smaller sails, but the hull shape is not stable—it is built for looks and speed. And wet fun (see Figure 7.3).

Figure 7.3.
(Photo courtesy of Dan Caplan Photography)

If a fast dinghy just will not do, a trailerable racing-cruising boat may be a great choice. Issues peculiar to trailerable boats are: How easily can the mast be raised and rigged, and how many people are needed to do that? Is a crane necessary? Writers have called the 1960s through the early 1980s the "golden age" of trailerable sailboats. Countless boats from that era in excellent condition capable of overnighting an entire family are available for very little cost. Some sell for less than $3,000. They age well because of their simplicity—there is little to go wrong that is difficult to fix. (Nevertheless, when budgeting, assume the boat will soon need new sails and a new outboard engine.) They tend to be lightly built, and, with little ballast, they are not designed for the open ocean. They can be great boats for learning on a small, quiet lake.

As you gain experience, these can be sailed on increasingly larger, more boisterous bodies of water—up to a point. Many have good sailing qualities and have safely sailed in such treacherous locales as the Great Lakes or seacoasts. Examples of inexpensive trailerable sailboats include Ventures (which were later renamed MacGregors), Lagunas, Santanas, San Juans, Schocks, Catalinas, and many others. Their abundance makes them inexpensive to buy. For example, there were 30,000 Venture 21s, 24s, and 25s built. Look for an airfoil-shaped retractable keel or centerboard (not a flat plate or shallow keel), one that can be raised for trailering. These provide upwind performance, yet allow for ramp launching. A retractable keel or centerboard is a great solution to the need for a deep keel yet shallow draft for launching, but those have compromises, too. They generally use up some interior space—sometimes a lot of interior space—for a structure to hold them. The need to retract them limits the amount of ballast in the keel. A retractable keel needs a device to hold the keel down; it should not rely on gravity alone.

As with all craft, check the integrity of the entire rig and its supporting base, and check for issues with the hull. In addition, check the pin the keel swings on and its attachment to the boat for integrity, rust, and corrosion. Rust on the iron keel itself is not a significant problem; it can be filed off. Check the operation and condition of the lifting cable and its winch.

Stereotyping boats by era

Certain eras of boat building had certain general characteristics. The boats of the 1960s to the mid-1970s, other than lightweight trailerables, were heavily built of solid fiberglass. Their fin keels were swept back. If they had a full-length keel, they tended to be slower and less maneuverable than their fin-keel cousins. Their hulls were narrower than today's boats, and their interior accommodations rarely stretched beneath the cockpit. The sailing rigs were shorter and wider than common now. The U. S.-built hull shapes were influenced by the Cruising Club of America (CCA) race handicap rule. The CCA era boats tend to look very pretty, with overhangs and pretty sheers. They tend to be comfortable cruisers. Many had inboard gasoline engines that have seen their youthful exuberance fade away; replacement is problematical.

The British had a different handicap rule. Boats built to one rule were not competitive under the other rule, so an International Offshore Rule (IOR) was created. Boats from the mid-1970s through the mid-1980s were influenced by the IOR and the gas crisis. Boats built with the IOR rule in mind were characterized by pinched ends. They were decent boats, but their lack of beam in the stern made them poor at carrying a spinnaker or travelling downwind. The mandates of the rule made the boats slower for their size than they needed to be. The IOR rule died in disgrace. Nonetheless, a retired IOR racer in good condition can be worth every penny. Some powerboat manufacturers switched to sailboats. Some were good, but many have dreadful sailing qualities.

Beginning in the 1970s and continuing to today, hulls were often not solid fiberglass. They were frequently built with a stiffening core of wood, which can rot, or foam, which can separate from the fiberglass. If in good condition, a cored hull can be a significant advantage; it is stiff, yet lightweight. A rotted or delaminated core will mean a costly and time-consuming repair.

Modern boats can be seen at any boat show. Attend a few, but your first boat should be selected for its responsiveness, not its accommodations. Go ahead and dream a little about that beautiful 50 foot well-equipped boat, but hold off for now.

Check the PHRF (Performance Handicap Racing Fleet) or Portsmouth Yardstick of any boat you are considering. These ratings compare speeds of different boats. Look it up on the Internet. Try to use your local area for the PHRF rating, since the PHRF will vary from location to location. If you are in a light-wind freshwater area, the PHRF rating for San Francisco Bay area salt water might be misleading. The Portsmouth rating is more appropriate for dinghies and small keelboats than PHRF. Your boat's Portsmouth rating may be found at http://www.ussailing.org/racing/offshore-big-boats/portsmouth-yardstick/portsmouth-yardstick-index/. The PHRF rating may be found at http://www.ussailing.org but may require logging in.

Length is a factor in speed. Again, physics controls. The speed of a wave in water divided by the square root of the wavelength (the separation between two waves) is a constant: 1.34 knots. At a speed faster than 1.34 knots times the square root of the waterline length of the boat, the boat will try to climb its own bow wave. This wastes the limited energy of the sails. So, unless you can get your boat to plane like a powerboat (which many dinghies and some larger boats can do), speed is limited by the length of your boat.

Trailering, mooring, and off-season storage

If you want to trailer your boat, first check to see how much weight your car can pull. Unless you want to shop for a new vehicle, your first boat including its trailer and equipment should weigh less than that. Almost all cars can pull 1,000 pounds; many standard-size cars, 2,000 pounds. Daysailers like Lightnings, Snipes, and Rebels can weigh under 1,000 pounds including the trailer. There are some camper-cruisers that with trailer weigh less than

1,000 pounds. If your car can haul 2,000 pounds, you can find a boat that sleeps four, like my Mirage 5.5. It is 1,200 pounds and, with its trailer and equipment, totals about 1,600 pounds. There are many examples of boats under 2,000 pounds including the trailer weight. Water ballast is an option for reducing tow weight. The maximum width for trailering is eight feet in some states, and 8 ½ feet in others. Permits are required for wider loads.

If your boat is not trailerable, you will need to obtain a mooring. Before buying a boat, learn what the availability and price is for mooring a boat of your chosen length, beam, and draft. What is the clearance of any relevant bridges? If there are shoals to cross, what is the maximum safe draft? Can the boat be stored in your driveway? If not, how much is off-season storage going to cost?

Determine the cost to bring the boat up to snuff

Consider the condition of the boat and the costs of any repairs, maintenance, upgrades, or replacement of missing parts. Replacing custom berth cushions is inexpensive but possibly challenging as a do-it-yourself project and expensive to have done for you. A missing mast can be replaced, but factor in shipping costs and the cost of rigging the new mast, as well as the purchase price of the mast itself. The condition of an engine can be a major factor. An outboard suitable for the average trailer sailor can be purchased brand new for well under $2,000 and can be transferred to another boat if you choose to. An inboard, even the smallest, needing to be rebuilt will cost at least $5,000, and a new inboard engine may cost perhaps $20,000 once shipping and installation are included.

Other issues in design and construction

Design and construction are major considerations. John Kretschmer, a well-known sailboat reviewer, will tell you that the importance of good design is so great it actually trumps the need for good construction. There are design parameters intended to help designers design and purchasers select. Although these have some value in comparing boats, they certainly have their limitations. These are usually expressed in dimensionless ratios, with standardized factors to allow the same ratio to have the same meaning in a 10-foot boat as a 100-foot boat. Sail area divided by displacement is important. A higher number is better in light winds. Remember these are generally optimal or theoretical. A furling sail will cut the actual sail area, sometimes a lot. Another is displacement over length; this will indicate performance. Lighter is faster, but a heavy boat can have a much more sea-kindly motion. Actual performance is also related to the location of the weight. Low is helpful (especially in the keel), high is harmful, and weight in the center of the boat is less harmful to performance than weight at the ends or sides. Generally length compared to width (beam) indicates simply if the boat is fat or thin; it doesn't tell you how far back the beam is carried. A beamy, light-weight boat might be great on smooth water, but it will have trouble going upwind in waves.

Other important ratios are *capsize screening formula* and *comfort ratio*. Wetted surface area is a dimension rarely given, but you can estimate it at a glance. The more surface in contact with the water, the more friction, and the slower the boat especially in light winds (as usual, this assumes all else is equal). The "prismatic coefficient," a formula rarely publicized, expresses this ratio. A high freeboard and high cabin have the effect of increasing air resistance, harming upwind performance, and making the boat a handful to moor or even anchor in a breeze. Dimensions important for cruisers include fuel and water capacity, holding-tank size, and number of berths useable at sea. A good description of many of these formulas can be found among other places at www.tedbrewer.com/yachtdesign.html. A handy calculator for some important ratios is available at www.image-ination.com/sailcalc.html.

The Mast

Does the boat have a masthead rig or a fractional rig? There are trade-offs. A masthead rig allows for more tension on the forestay. Since the jib is attached to the forestay, the greater tension allows for a straighter jib, which helps the boat go upwind. Since the genoa goes to the top of the mast, it can be bigger. A masthead rig will have a shorter, easier-to-raise mast than a fractional rig for the same sail area, and the more sail area, the faster the boat can become. A fractionally rigged boat (the jib goes partway or a large fraction of the way to the top of the mast) will better allow the mast to bend, helping control the mainsail's shape. It also will tend to have a larger mainsail, which improves sailing performance under main alone. This can be a huge benefit sailing in the tight quarters typically found in a marina. A trailerable boat, other than a racing boat, should have the mast start at deck level. This makes it easier to raise and eliminates a leaky hole in the cabin.

What is underneath counts a lot

Consider all of the boat's wings: its keel, rudder, and sails. A deep keel means your boat cannot be launched on most ramps. A shallow keel means performance, particularly upwind, is seriously compromised. Wing keels got great publicity when Australia won the America's Cup with a wing keel. However, that was a deep wing keel. It was so deep in fact that an attempt was made to disqualify the boat, because, when heeled, its depth was greater than permitted. A boat with only a shallow keel, even one with a wing, may disappoint. ". . . remember, there is no substitute for draft when it comes to performance" (Robert Perry, *Sailing Designs*, Volume 6, page 66). Perry, who is among the top naval architects of our times, was speaking of cruising boats when he wrote this. It is not just the racer who should optimize performance.

The cabin

The interior design of a boat is a matter of personal choice. It is important to understand the effect those personal choices have on your finances, your use of the boat, and your fun. Issues related to the head, such as the number of compartments; their size (Do you fit inside it? Can you turn around inside it with the door closed?); and whether there is pressure water, hot water, and a shower are all personal choices. Some personal choices add to sailing pleasure; others can seriously hinder performance. You should understand that the weight and swelling of the hull caused by a wonderful interior may be the cause of a not-so-wonderful sailing experience.

If you want a larger cruising boat, think carefully about what you need and especially what you do not need. For example, if you only weekend aboard, you do not need a refrigerator. If you do not have an electrical hookup at your mooring, your refrigerator will be warm when you arrive and will quickly drain the battery as it cools. Food stowage and preparation are beyond the scope of this book, but Beth Leonard wrote an excellent article for the January 2009 edition of *Cruising World,* in which she describes how to live without refrigeration. Her answer is: easily, and well.

If your boat is twice the size you need, your sails will be at least twice as heavy to hoist. Okay, roller furling can compensate. But you will have twice as much to paint, twice as much to repair, and twice the storage fees both winter and summer. You can, however, be host to twice as many people. That is a better choice for your next boat.

Can you actually sleep in the bunk under way? A lot of boats feature an owner's cabin underneath the cockpit, with a double bed centered in the owner's cabin. Very nice, but do not even think about sleeping there while under way. It may be the first time in the history of that common dream that you do not wake up before you land.

Why is full standing headroom hard to achieve on a well-performing boat under 30 feet? Physics, again. Poetry also. Physics says the high sides have greater wind resistance. Also, the higher the cabin top, the higher the sails, and the higher the sails, the more they will tip the boat over in a breeze. Therefore, the higher the cabin, the smaller the sails and slower the boat. Poetry says the higher the sides, the harder it is to make the boat shapely. For some reason, a good sailing boat will also look good, just like airplanes that look right generally fly right. Smaller boats with excellent sailing qualities may have only sitting headroom in the cabin.

Calling the plumber

Most harbors have bathroom facilities. Still, for many an enclosed head is essential for overnighting with unrelated people. For daysailing, the entire cabin can be the enclosed head. But what if it rains? Can everyone go someplace dry while a guest uses the facilities with some privacy? Do you really want a flush toilet instead of a porta-potty in that enclosed head? Picture calling a plumber on your cell phone asking him to come 10 miles out to sea before you decide a flush toilet is a necessity. Understand what a disaster it is to have just a small leak in flexible hoses running to and especially from the toilet. Understand, too, that the toilet hoses in a boat trap gunk, and, to some extent, the odor penetrates through the hose. It is enough to make you give up boating. The porta-potty, imperfect as it may be, does have advantages. It is ironic that the talented and knowledgeable sailboat critic who most disagrees with this is named John.

Dinner call

Do you really want to cook aboard or just carry sandwiches and go to restaurants? You have to really love to cook to attempt it in any pleasure craft. The rocking and small space is a challenge to the soufflé makers. The cook may rightfully demand standing headroom in the galley. It may be created in your craft with a pop-open top or hatch. These are nice but frequently leak.

Look for a stove and oven intended for marine use. It must be gimbaled if it is to be used under way. Even when moored, it must have clamps to secure any hot pots or pans. Otherwise, they could spill. Secure lids are a must. There are many fuel types to choose from. Each type of fuel has its advantages and disadvantages.

Any table needs a high edge, called a *fiddle*, which will keep the tableware from becoming cabinware.

At anchor

Is the boat set up for easy anchoring? The anchor can be secured on deck with chocks or stowed in an anchor locker. A windlass can be used to grip and ease or haul the anchor line or chain. Easy anchoring involves a sturdy bow roller holding the anchor securely, a windlass, and a chain locker below to hold the anchor line. All this involves a lot of weight at an end of the boat, which does not help performance. You will not see such an arrangement on a boat oriented for speed, or on many cruiser-racers.

An important feature of an interior is ventilation. In warm climates, you will need more ventilation than in colder climes. Be sure you have enough for comfort. Can the ventilation be used in a seaway? Most opening hatches and ports must be closed when conditions deteriorate. Air-conditioning usually requires a shore-power (110-volt) connection.

A great addition to any boat, sail or power, is a solar-powered vent. Some have a battery that gets charged by the solar panel, so they really do run 24-7. They do not have a great deal of power, but through constant work, they move a lot of air in a day, do not drain your boat's battery, require minimal maintenance, and cost nothing to operate. They will keep your boat dry and fresh smelling. The vent is generally waterproof, but, in case of a serious sea condition, the vent opening can be filled with the included plug.

Guidebooks about available sailboats

John Kretschmer has written several books and countless articles about cruising boats and cruising itself. Robert Perry has his articles, at least 1,500 of them, that can be found in no less than six large books entitled *Sailing Designs*. John Kretschmer writes about and favors boats that are available in large numbers and are good long-distance cruisers. These tend to be 30 feet and longer, with some exceptions. His analyses include defects that arose over time with a particular production boat. Robert Perry likes boats of any size that sail well and look good. Who could argue with that? With his designer's eye, Perry can judge a boat's sailing qualities at a glance. His reviews analyze and explain what is right and wrong about a design. This can be very useful information when you choose to purchase your own boat.

Sailing magazine hosts Perry and other sailboat reviewers. *Sail* has some wonderful articles. My favorite contributor to *Sail* is Nigel Calder, whose coverage of electrical and mechanical issues aboard is excellent. He learned his lessons the hard way so you can learn yours the easy way. *Small Craft Advisor*, *Good Old Boat*, and the late *Small Boat Journal* cover well the under-30-foot boats. There are a number of excellent magazines devoted to the cruising crowd, such as *Blue Water Sailor* and *Cruising World*.

Singlehanding and sail controls

One sailing quality that can be evaluated at the dock or even on land is how adaptable a boat is to singlehanding. To be a good singlehander, or a good boat for a couple that will allow one person to keep watch, the frequently used controls must be reachable with one hand on the helm. Are the engine controls right there? Can you reach the sheet winches? Are the winches self-tailing? Is there a quick, safe, easy path to other controls? How about docking? Can all the cleats be easily reached, or at least is there a stern or springline cleat very easily reached by the skipper? Sometimes you must step away from the helm. Does it have an autopilot, wind vane steering, or both? Or perhaps it has just a rope to tie the tiller or wheel in one position.

While we are on the subject of reaching controls, the skipper should be able to stand on the cockpit seats, raising himself for a better view while controlling steering, especially in the harbor. He should also be able to sit on the desired side, for a better view while the boat is heeling. Tillers accommodate this easily. Wheels may not. A large wheel is one solution; another is twin wheels. This brings us in turn to access to the transom, for swimming, recovery of swimmers, docking, and boarding in general. A solution is for the designer to remove most of the transom. This allows water to drain quickly, but loose items will be carried swiftly away as well. This feature is found more often in racing boats than cruisers. On such a boat, keep your dog on a leash and yourself on a tether. An extension pole is usually fitted to a tiller. One can also be fitted to a wheel.

Multihulls

How many hulls do you want? This is a fundamental question, not a silly one. Monohulls are traditional; catamarans and trimarans are less so, having two and three hulls, respectively. Catamarans and trimarans rely on width, or beam, to keep from tipping over. Monohulls rely on a ballasted keel. Monohulls will heel more but have less tendency to tip completely over and a greater capacity to recover if they do.

Catamarans can use that entire beam to have a great cabin without the loss of performance that an excessively beamy monohull will have. This is simply because that beam's surface is divided in two hulls, with no surface dragging along in between. Often, a cat will be slowed by all the weight aboard. Cats seem to respond more poorly to excess weight than do monohulls. They often have poor, nearly nonexistent keels, so they do not sail upwind well. Trimarans can be great trailering boats. Lacking ballast, they are lighter and easier to tow than comparable monohulls. For the same reason, they can sail faster as well. If the outer hulls are retractable, a common feature in tris, the overall width can be made legal for highways. Many are designed so that can be quickly and easily done. Catamarans that have the cabin extend from one hull to another can very rarely be designed to retract to a narrow enough package to tow legally. Catamarans can be much faster than traditional craft downwind. Trimarans can sail fast upwind or down, but the cabin size is reduced.

You will be able to find a boat that sails well *and* has a nice interior. Before you buy, hire a competent yacht surveyor. Get yourself a good sailing boat. Have fun. Enjoy the style, the breezes, the sights at your own time and pace. Develop your skills. Be safe; always sail within your capabilities, stretching them slowly, carefully, and knowledgeably.

Thank you

Thank you for reading this book. It is the product of years of work. It was written for you, and for sailors worldwide. I hope it has broadened your horizons and led you to many years of many destinations.

It is time to return to a thought from the beginning of this book. A key to safe sailing is to stay within your developing abilities. Another is to continually develop your abilities so you can deal with the unanticipated.

You, and you alone, as captain of your vessel are solely responsible for the safety of yourself, all those aboard, and those who may be called upon to rescue you if you get into trouble.

This book could have been thousands of pages long and still not covered everything you could use to sail well. I'll leave you with several appendices and the advice to keep learning and keep your eyes and ears open. It is said that, "It is a poor workman who blames his tools." Your tools include your ship, your charts, your sails, your electronics, and the weather. No matter what they, your tools, may do, you cannot blame them. You must use them to insure the safety and security of your craft, your company, and others who may be affected by it, and, when they fail, you must be prepared to carry on. You must take the attitude that it is your job to maintain the boat, and any failure of the boat is a failure of you, the captain, to keep it operating properly.

At the beginning of Day Six appeared the quote, "It is not the ship so much as the skillful sailing that assures the [successful] sailing." George William Curtis. Do not just read that and quote it. Live it, and you will live well.

May fair winds follow you all your days.

APPENDIX A

MARINE FIRST AID

The author thanks John Williams and John Graneto, experienced emergency room physicians at University of Illinois Hospital and Swedish Covenant Hospital, respectively, in Chicago, Illinois, for information on the most common shipboard first-aid issues.

FALLS. Suppose a middle-aged person falls and hits his head. Check for equal pupil size and reaction. Check to see if he is moving all extremities. You want to make sure he didn't fall because of a stroke. If he had a stroke, he is likely to need emergency attention as soon as possible. There is roughly a three-hour window for giving certain medications. Classical signs of a stroke include weakness on one side, slurred speech or difficulty speaking, confusion, vision changes, difficulty walking, and dizziness, with or without a headache. Persons with those symptoms should rest while others rush to obtain medical services for him. If symptoms aren't obvious, test for symptoms of stroke. Ask the person to smile. Does his smile look different? Ask the person to speak an entire sentence coherently. Have the person raise both hands. Can the person stick his tongue out straight? Call 911 or the Coast Guard on channel 16 immediately if you have any doubts about his condition.

If a person falls from being struck by an object, the good news is it wasn't a stroke. Check frequently for alertness, coherence, and equal pupil dilation and reaction to light. If in any doubt, contact the authorities for assistance.

CUTS. It is no longer recommended to use an antiseptic. The common antiseptics cause too much damage to healthy tissue adjacent to the wound. Use clear water instead to flush the wound out. To stop the bleeding, apply continuous pressure on the wound for two to five minutes.

SEVERE SUNBURN. Like any burn, cool the affected area with water. Get the person into shade as soon as possible. Give the person a drink. Water is best; I also recommend coconut water for general hydration. Dark drinks can be diuretics. Alcohol does not help. Solarcain is a pain killer similar to Lidocain and Novocain. It makes the person feel better; it does not promote healing.

NAUSEA. This can be deceptive. It could be simple seasickness, but it could be something else. If the boat has a gas engine or generator, be concerned about carbon monoxide poisoning. Get the person on deck; do not allow anyone to remain below decks without checking on that person. A diesel engine is unlikely to generate significant amounts of carbon monoxide. Watch for dehydration; provide water. Anticipate seasickness; at the first queasiness get on deck and take ginger ale or a cola and saltines. Do not take a seasickness remedy just as a precaution before your first sail. It can make you very sleepy. If you must take a seasickness remedy as a precaution, try it beforehand to learn its side effects on dry land; don't drive.

FISHHOOKS AND SPLINTERS. The person giving aid and the one receiving aid should position themselves so that the aid giver can see clearly what is to be done, and the person

Figure 8.0.

receiving aid is kept from viewing the work, which should prevent the victim from flinching. Because the boat is rocking, it is best for both to be pressed against a bulkhead. See the photo as an example.

A fishhook should never be pulled out in a manner that allows the barb to reenter the skin. If the hook is exposed on both ends, cut off either end, and pull the hook out following the pathway of its entrance. Otherwise, pad it properly to reduce pain and keep it from moving; then get that person medical attention.

HYPOTHERMIA. Hypothermia is a dangerous condition. A person loses body heat much more quickly in cold water than in cold air. When the body gets cold, symptoms can begin with mental confusion or an inability to react, and proceed to death in less than an hour in 50-degree water. A quick rescue and warm dry clothing are essential. If someone is seriously hypothermic, that person is likely to exhibit confusion and may have stopped shivering. Warm only the trunk of a seriously hypothermic person, as warming the extremities may send dangerously cold blood to the heart and brain.

CARDIAC ARREST. Check and clear the airway. If unsure if there is a pulse, apply pressure to the chest using both hands intertwined. Push and release about two inches deep (for adults; less for children) on an area between the nipples. Rescue (mouth-to-mouth) breathing is no longer considered essential but may be done at the rate of two breaths every 30 pushes. The pushes are done at the rate of 100 per minute, a little less than two times per second. The idea is to create a life-sustaining pulse. As with any serious medical condition, do everything necessary to quickly get the victim medical assistance.

Heart attack symptoms may not be the classical feeling like "an elephant is on my chest." They may be more vague (particularly in women), such as sudden and severe fatigue, nausea, shortness of breath, or dizziness, even without chest pain. If any doubt, call 911 or the Coast Guard on channel 16 for expert advice.

SAILING EMERGENCIES

The U.S. Coast Guard has implemented "Rescue 21" in all major sailing areas of the coasts and Great Lakes of the lower 48 states, with more areas soon to be covered. This provides for faster rescues of properly registered craft, so it is vitally important that you register your electronics.

As skipper/owner, your job is to register your boat's emergency radio equipment. For offshore work, an Emergency Position Indicating Radio Beacon (EPIRB) can be purchased or even rented. This is a device that can typically be activated manually or automatically by immersion in water. It sends a signal to satellites, which then alert rescuers. If it is equipped with a GPS, it will more quickly tell rescuers your exact location. There are various types of personal locators, such as SPOT™, which like EPIRBs are only effective if registered to the owner. A DSC-equipped marine radio is highly recommended. It is a standard marine radio whose range is typically only 15 to 25 miles but with Digital Selective Calling (DSC). The DSC-equipped radio, properly registered, will notify rescuers of your boat name, type, and ownership and provide contact information so authorities will (hopefully) quickly learn that the emergency call is valid. Make sure your DSC-equipped radio has a GPS properly connected to it. Some have integrated GPS, others a connection to an independent GPS. Properly connected to a GPS and with the radio registered, your exact location and distress will be broadcast to rescuers. The procedure for registration may vary. For example, Boat U.S. will register your DSC radio for free, but this registration is only valid in the United States. It is estimated that 80 percent of all such electronics in use are not properly registered. This is dangerous; it will delay rescue. Who wants that? Not the people in need of rescue and not those who are searching, because every minute of search creates risk.

CREW OVERBOARD

Learning and practicing crew-overboard procedures is an important skill for all crew to be completely familiar with. See the twelfth step in Day Three for a full discussion.

STEERING DIFFICULTIES

IF THE RUDDER BREAKS OR JAMS. There are actually several solutions to this problem besides the obvious, an emergency rudder, which most of you will not have. Your boat is likely to have a mainsail behind the mast and a jib in front. The jib in front will tend to turn the boat away from the wind, because it is in front of the point the boat will spin around (the center of the keel). The main, behind the keel, will tend to force the boat to turn into the wind. A complicating factor is that the more the boat leans to the side, the more it will tend to turn into the wind.

TO USE THE SAILS TO STEER. To turn away from the wind, keep the jib in the wind, and let the mainsail "weathervane." The mainsail will offer the least resistance it can to the wind and the jib in front, the most. The result is that the boat will turn away from the wind. To turn toward the wind, let the jib weathervane, and keep the mainsail in, moving the boat forward and turning it (into the wind). Develop some subtlety to your sail handling, and the boat will reward you by remaining in better control.

DRILL. Tie down the wheel or tiller. This will help you go straight, of course, but your objective is to steer without using it. Later, try it with the rudder looser so it can wiggle a bit. This will be a more difficult test of your rudderless steering.

Start by pulling in the sails a little bit at a time. Try to move them both about the same amount in order to keep the boat moving straight.

You can try running the engine, if you have enough fuel to get to your destination. See how the boat moves under the engine. Can you keep going generally straight, or turn by suddenly reversing or accelerating the engine? Can you continue to do that with the rudder allowed to wiggle a bit? Probably you will need the sails to help you turn.

A boat without a rudder can be steered by any means that drags more on one side of the boat than the other. An oar can be rigged to use as a combination rudder and tiller. Tie it securely; you do not want to lose it. You could drag a long line from the stern. Attach to it lines running to each of two winches, one on each side, forming a shape like the letter *Y*. Crank in on one side, and the line moves that way, causing its drag on one side of the boat to turn the boat toward that side. This is something to experiment with, but be aware that the line can get wrapped around the propeller. If so, your engine cannot run and may be wrecked.

If you have an outboard, you have a huge advantage over an inboard, because you can turn the outboard engine as desired to steer. Practice this.

Which direction should you head in? If you are anticipating no serious weather, head away from a shore you could get blown into. Then, practice your boat handling until you feel confident with it. Only then, head to a harbor, preferably one to windward—if your engine fails, you will have time to get assistance, and the waves will diminish as you approach the windward shore—or anchor and await a tow.

RIGGING PROBLEMS

Let's suppose your mast falls over. Cut it away as necessary, or secure it so it doesn't punch a hole in the hull. Bear in mind your boat will rock much more when the mast is down or missing. Seasickness is a real possibility here, but get the boat safe before taking an anti-nausea drug that may make you drowsy. Drink some ginger ale or cola, and eat some saltines to reduce seasickness as soon as the boat is not in immediate danger of being holed.

If you lose your mast, you can still create a jury-rig. I can only generalize here. Examine your assets: Is there a large section of mast left unbent? If so, cut off the unbent portion from the damaged part with a hacksaw, and stabilize it with lines between its top and strong points on the boat. Rig a sail or sails. Sometimes the sails will fit sideways if you move the bottom part of the sail to the vertical. If the mast is hopeless, perhaps a spinnaker pole can be used in place of a mast. Be sure to run a potential halyard or two—or three—through the top before raising the pole.

ENGINE DIFFICULTIES

Be sure the fuel tank doesn't have gunk in it at the bottom. There are services and means to clean diesel fuel. It is called *polishing* the fuel. Any gunk will float free in rough conditions and can clog the fuel filter. Be prepared to change filter cartridges quickly. Diesel engines are more prone to this type of problem than gasoline engines, because bacteria are more likely to grow in the moisture in diesel fuel than in gasoline.

Gasohol causes more difficulties in boats than cars. This is because the fuel in a boat might sit unused long enough to degrade. As the fuel in the tank sits, it can absorb moisture past its ability to hold it. This causes the fuel and the alcohol to separate, causing starting and running issues. Fuel can, over time, coat the sensitive carburetor and other parts, again causing running difficulties.

Fuel stabilizers are a great help in both diesel and gasoline engine performance. Add some to your tank per the engine manufacturer's recommendation.

HEAVY WEATHER

While preparing for heavy weather is beyond the scope of this book, generally speaking sailing in heavy weather requires reducing sail area and flattening sails. You can switch to a smaller jib, reef the mainsail, lower the jib entirely, set a storm trysail, or remove all sails and even go below, letting the boat fend for itself. The latter is undesirable in the extreme, but sometimes it is more dangerous to have someone on the deck, exposed to the wind and waves.

With the boat rocking in the large waves, any debris in the bottom will move around and possibly gravitate to the bilge pumps. Keep the bilge clear. To the extent you didn't, be ready to clear the pumps or to use a bucket.

If ashore, clear the deck of sails and gear. Add chafing gear to any areas of mooring lines that could abrade.

FLYING A SPINNAKER

Your boat will cover a lot of territory quickly when under spinnaker. That is why we have learned to read charts and sail to another harbor first. You need to know where the obstructions are. You also do not have right-of-way simply because you are using a spinnaker. Often, nearly the opposite is true.

Spinnakers can be flown on a given tack using the same basic techniques as with a jib, but the spinnaker is a bit more temperamental. This is both because the spinnaker is larger and because, unlike the jib, which is secured along an entire edge, it is secured only at three points, and those not completely. The spinnaker is secured only near the mast with its halyard, a sheet, and at its own special boom, called a *spinnaker pole*, connected to the spinnaker with a line (called a *guy*).

SPINNAKER GEAR AND HANDLING

The big difference between adjusting a jib and flying a spinnaker has to do with placing and adjusting the spinnaker pole. There are two basic types of spinnakers: asymmetrical and symmetrical.

Setting and Handling the Spinnaker Pole

The spinnaker pole is set just before the spinnaker is hoisted. Asymmetrical and symmetrical spinnakers have different types of poles, described below. It is possible to save some effort and simply attach the tack (front edge) of the spinnaker to the bow of the boat using a short lanyard. The shape of the spinnaker will not be optimal, but you will get some benefit from the sail in the right conditions.

ASYMMETRICAL SPINNAKERS. An asymmetrical spinnaker uses a pole mounted on the deck, which may need to be moved forward with control lines.

SYMMETRICAL SPINNAKERS. The symmetrical spinnaker uses a pole more complicated to set:

1. You must first secure yourself on the foredeck. Take a wide, comfortable, and, most importantly, secure stance. Wedge your back into the mast and wires to help secure yourself. At points you will need both hands for the pole (one on the pole itself, the other sometimes releasing and reconnecting the guy). A tether is highly recommended when working the foredeck of a keelboat. Be sure that however you have secured yourself, you can free yourself in the event of an emergency.

2. Look at the pole. It has a fitting on a wire to be attached to a line that will pull it up, and another to hold it down. These are called the *uphaul* and *downhaul*. It also has two clips, one at each end, often called *jaws*. Usually these are identical and face the same direction, so the pole can be set with the jaws up or down. The clips are opened by pulling on a line so the crew doesn't have to reach to the end of the pole. Usually, each clip has its own line. See how it opens and closes (it is spring loaded so it closes tight automatically). See also how light the pole is, considering its size and strength. Look on the mast for a ring or device to connect the pole to the mast. Be very sure you are using the correct fittings.

3. Hook up the uphaul and downhaul so the jaws face in the proper direction. Usually the jaws face up, so that the pole could just drop away when the jaws are opened, but this is considered a matter of personal preference (skipper's choice). See which lines to use, and where and how they are adjusted and cleated.

4. Using the line on the pole, open the jaw and connect it to the line that goes to the spinnaker. That line will now be called the "guy" as in "guy wire". Be sure you have connected the pole to the guy on the proper side of the forestay. The pole will stick out on the side opposite the sail, not the same side as the sail.

5. Once the pole is connected to the guy, connect it to the mast, using the fitting attached to the mast for that purpose.

6. Adjust the height of the pole. The pole has two lines attached. One pulls the pole up, the other down. When the spinnaker is full and drawing, the pole will want to rise. The downhaul controls that. The uphaul holds the pole when there is no wind, or when jibing the pole. Set the pole height so that the pole side of the spinnaker is the same height off the deck (not the water) as the other corner (the "clew"). Your skipper's preference may change this.

7. Adjust the angle of the pole. The pole can be moved forward and back with the "guy." Its basic position is to be perpendicular to the wind. Never let it strike the forestay, which can damage it or the pole.

Handling the pole during a jibe

Jibing a spinnaker is often called *tacking*, although in this book we use the term tacking for bringing the bow through the direction of the wind, and jibing for bringing the stern through the direction of the wind.

You must first secure yourself on the foredeck.

1. To perform an *end-for-end jibe*, have the pole's uphaul and downhaul loosened enough so you can move it. In coordination with the helmsman, when the boat is approaching the straight downwind point or when you can soonest make the connections properly, release the guy, release the pole from the mast, and move it sideways so the end that was on the mast can now connect up with the old sheet (which now becomes the guy) and then connect the other side to the mast.

2. A *dip pole jibe* is used on larger sailboats, ones whose pole is too heavy to handle in an end-for-end jibe. A dip-pole jibe often requires raising the end of the pole fitted to the mast. There is usually a control line for that purpose. If a dip pole jibe is used, the pole end set into the mast is raised and the end at the guy is lowered so it will pass behind the forestay. Reconnect the old sheet, which becomes the new guy on the other side of the boat, raise the pole at the guy, and lower the end attached to the mast.

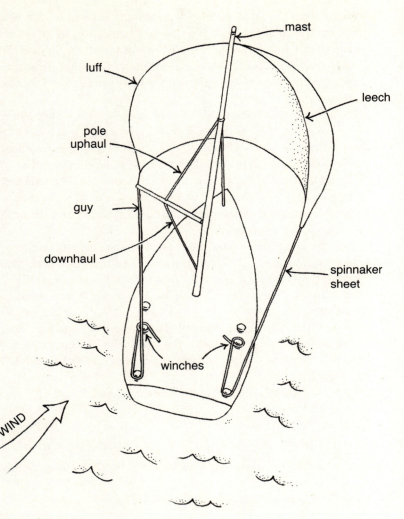

Figure 8.1. (Drawing by Christopher Hoyt)

mast

luff

leech

pole
uphaul

guy

downhaul

spinnaker
sheet

winches

WIND

Wow! Great jibe.

Raising the spinnaker

Once the pole is set, the spinnaker can be raised:

1. Place the spinnaker bag, with the spinnaker ready, on the proper side of the boat. This will be the leeward side once on the intended heading. Attach the spinnaker bag to the boat.
2. Both sheets and a halyard must first be attached to the spinnaker. One sheet is led through a fitting at the end of the spinnaker pole.

When given the signal pull on that sheet until the spinnaker nearly touches the pole. That "sheet" gets a new name, the guy. It has to be long. Before the spinnaker is hoisted, it runs from the spinnaker, around outside all of the stays and shrouds, to a turning block at the stern, and then to the trimmer, the crew handling the sheet and guy.

3. The halyard must be attached to the head of the spinnaker. Place a swivel at the head, or use clear markings, to distinguish the head easily from the clews. Usually, the head has a red and green edge tape adjacent. The clews usually have a white tape and a red or green adjacent. When you are rushed, this may not be a sufficient distinction.

4. The sheet and guy are usually run to turning blocks on each side deck very near the transom.

5. Raise the spinnaker. Untie the spinnaker bag's closure so the spinnaker can come out of the bag. Pull on the spinnaker halyard raising the sail until it is very near the mast. If too low it will move around too much, but with some experience, you could lower it a foot or two to get it clearer from the disturbed air off the mainsail. Sometimes the sail fills so much with air you cannot hoist it high enough. If so, ease the sheet (the line not going to the pole or to the mast) to spill some air, or connect the halyard to a winch.

6. "Sheet in." Adjust the sheet as described below.

Jibing the symmetrical spinnaker: handling the lines

Jibing downwind is coordinated with turning the boat and handling the pole.

The steps to spinnaker line handling in a jibe:

1. Sheet out—a lot, in coordination with the turning of the boat, so the spinnaker stays filled with air. The person handling the pole will have work to do. The pole must be moved from one side of the boat to the other and disconnected from one spinnaker sheet and connected to the other.

2. Try to make the job easier for the crew handling the pole. You may have to loosen the uphaul and downhaul a bit so the pole can be maneuvered. You may ask how loose he wants it before the jibe.

3. Once the pole has been moved to the other side of the boat and is secure in the new guy and the mast, using the new guy pull the spinnaker within a couple of inches of the pole, then set up the pole and sheet as before. Often this will be the mirror image of before. Let the guy out or pull in the guy to adjust the pole's position, making it perpendicular to the wind, and probably sheet in.
4. (Meanwhile, the helmsperson tries to coordinate the turn with the crew's work, so that the pole handler moves the pole over to its new position, and the new guy is properly attached, before the turn is completed.)

Congratulations—Great Jibe!

Coordinating steering with your crew using the spinnaker

The skipper should:

1. Move the rudder to turn the boat downwind in the desired direction.
2. Call for the spinnaker hoisting.
3. Changing headings will change speed and affect heeling. Turning the boat a bit upwind will speed the boat up but increase heeling. Call "heading up" to alert the crew to adjust the spinnaker and prepare for the boat to heel. Call "heading down" when you desire to reduce the angle of heel and turn the boat more downwind.
4 Use a steady hand when jibing. Turn slowly enough through the jibe that your crew can keep up. Pause your turn to proceed straight downwind if the pole has not yet been connected to the new guy. Shout "great job" when done.

Adjusting the spinnaker

As trimmer, the person handling the sheet, you will follow the same rules as with any jib: when in doubt, let it out. Let it out until it just luffs, then pull it in until it just fills. It is okay to let the spinnaker luff just a little, having just a small curl.

The asymmetrical spinnaker works better when the wind is a little more off to the side. The symmetrical is at its best more directly downwind.

As the trimmer, you may be asked to adjust the guy so that the pole remains perpendicular to the wind, and to adjust the height of the pole using the uphaul and downhaul.

Dousing the spinnaker

Dousing the spinnaker is taking it down and stowing it, ready to be used again. The leeward takedown is easiest. To reduce confusion, only the leeward dousing is described below:

1. If racing, before dousing the spinnaker the appropriate foresail is selected, sheets attached, and raised.
2. The trimmer loosens the guy until the spinnaker flutters off to leeward.
3. The sheet is taken in by hand by the foredeck crew, leading to a good grip on that corner of the spinnaker itself. The spinnaker continues to be hauled in by hand in coordination with the halyard being lowered by the trimmer at a pace such that the spinnaker neither lands in the water nor resists the efforts of those pulling it down. It is frequently lowered directly into the cabin as it is being hauled in.
4. The sheet, guy, and halyard are removed from the sail. The halyard must be secured to the boat as soon as it is detached from the spinnaker.
5. Each of the three edges (foot, luff, and leech, or foot and two luffs) usually has an edge reinforcing tape of a contrasting color; this helps you identify it. Also locate both bottom corners (clews), which have holes to attach the sheet and guy. It is essential to leave both clews as well as the head (top) of the spinnaker sticking out of the bag, so that lines can be attached quickly.
6. Begin putting the sail into its bag, starting with the foot (bottom edge). Start at the center of the foot and work it along the edge from there, not one half at a time, but both halves at the same pace.
7. After the foot is in, one luff's edge is inserted into the bag, working from bottom to top, remembering to leave the hole in the head of the spinnaker sticking out so the halyard can be quickly attached. (There should be a clear indication on the sail which hole is for the halyard; otherwise, the sail could be raised sideways.) Do the same with the remaining edge. (Some skippers believe only one luff tape must be inserted before the body of the sail, while others insist on both.)

8. The rest of the spinnaker can usually just be stuffed in, but avoid twisting the sail as it is stuffed in the bag.

In that manner, the spinnaker is stowed so it can be put away or hoisted again soon.

CRUISING BOAT GEAR

Current U.S. Coast Guard required equipment is found in their publication *A Boater's Guide to the Federal Requirements for Recreational Boats*. It can be found on the Internet, free of charge, at http://www.uscgboating.org/assets/1/workflow_staging/Publications/420. PDF. Boaters without the minimum equipment are subject to large fines or worse.

Those, however, are the minimum requirements. My recommendations are different for different classes of vessels. This is a list of proposed gear for vessels that will not be out of VHF ship-to-shore range for more than the briefest of times. Serious cruising requires additional equipment.

A dinghy includes all sailboats without an engine or cabin. Usually lacking lights, they are not to be sailed at night. Cruising-class boats are any boat with an engine: inboard, gas or diesel, or outboard.

Any electronics list will be out of date by the time of publication. Accordingly, there is no attempt to discuss chart plotters, depth sounders, or other electronics beyond the most basic. For the latest and greatest electronics, check out the Technology Awards given out by the National Marine Electronics Association, or the annual roundup by many sailing magazines.

Some of the heavier spare equipment for maintaining a boat can be left ashore.

FLOTATION AND RECOVERY OF SWIMMERS

Gear	Boat Type
A PFD for every person aboard	All
A throwable floatation device	All except the smallest dinghies
A means to hoist a swimmer aboard. *This can be a swim ladder or a more complex device.*	All except the smallest dinghies

HULL (TO PREVENT SINKING)

Gear	Boat Type
A plug for every through-hull fitting (attached to each through-hull)	All
Large, soft foam (to plug other holes)	All
Hose clamps of various sizes	All with any hoses
Bilge pump(s)	Per size of boat.
Sponge	All
Bucket	All except dinghies with small self-bailing cockpits, such as the Sunfish and Laser

TOOLS

Gear	Boat Type
Channel locks	Cruising class
Vise Grips	Cruising class
Crescent wrench	Cruising class
Screwdrivers, Phillips and flat, various	Cruising class
Hacksaw	Cruising class
Knife	All: A small folding pocket knife for each crew, attached with a lanyard
Drill	Desirable

NAVIGATION

Gear	Boat Type/Conditions
Charts of all relevant areas	All (stored at home for dinghies)
Parallel ruler, pencil, ruler, compass	All (stored at home for dinghies)
Navigation lights (sometimes called running lights)	All night operations
Replacement bulbs	All night operations
Dim red light to illuminate charts, etc.	All night operations
Compass, one either hand-held or fixed	All
Compass, one fixed and one hand-held	Cruising class
Wind speed and wind direction indicator	Desirable
Boat speed indicator	Desirable
Depth sounder	Cruising class
GPS (marine) with MOB button	All except dinghies
Binoculars	All except dinghies. 7x50 recommended. That is a magnification of 7, and 50-millimeter front lenses.
Night vision monocular	Desirable for night sailing. Presently still expensive.
Radar	Desirable
Radar reflector	Recommended for all night sailing and all cruising class
Chart plotter, connecting all navigation gear	Desirable
Replacement fuses	Cruising class

WEATHER

Gear	Boat Type
Weather radio receiver	All; one with a weather alarm is desirable
Barometer	Cruising class. A recording instrument is recommended.
Internet sources for weather	Strongly recommended

STEERING

Gear	Boat Type
Replacement parts	Cruising class
Emergency rudder	Recommended. Required gear in certain races.
Mechanical steering	All

This can range from a simple tie-down for the tiller to self-steering gear to an autopilot, depending on the length of time one needs to be away from the tiller.

ROPES, SAILS, AND MOORING

Gear	Boat Type
Anchor and rode	Cruising class
Dock lines (four) and three fenders	Cruising class
Sail repair tape	Cruising class
Spare shackles	Cruising class
Spare turning blocks	Cruising class
Spare winch handle	Cruising class
Winch repair kit	Cruising class
Grease, oil, springs, and pawls	Cruising class
Boat hook	Cruising class

COOKING

Food and water for twice the   Per choice of sailor
anticipated sailing duration   All

SIGNALING

Gear	Boat Type
Sounding device (horn or bell)	Cruising class
Whistle	All; one for each person aboard
Personal light, flashlight	All nighttime, one for each person aboard
Flares, 3 minimum	Cruising class
Marine radio, fixed and handheld	Cruising class
Mirror, signaling	Cruising class
AIS (automatic identification system)	Desirable, cruising class
Cell phone	All, in waterproof case
Personal locator (Personal GPS)	Desirable

WATERPROOF CONTAINERS

All; sized to protect phones, cameras, changes of clothing.

PADDLE

Some small cruising class may use one   Dinghies
   as a spare.

ENGINE SPARES AND TOOL REQUIREMENTS

Consult your engine manufacturer and fellow sailors for the specific items that frequently fail on your engine. If they suggest water pumps on your engine are prone to failure, order one now. Otherwise, you may find your engine out of action for weeks awaiting that part. Parts for boat engines are not as readily available as they are for cars.

Generally, you will want to have the following:

Gear	Boat Type
Filters	Cruising class
Impeller	Cruising class
Oil	Cruising class
Wire brush	Cruising class
Battery charger	Cruising class
Inverter	Cruising class
Spare wire	Cruising class
Spark plugs	Cruising class with gas engines
Fire extinguishers	Cruising class. Per U.S. Coast Guard requirements: one, two, or more.

PAPERS

Documents	Boat Type
Ownership papers	All (stored at home for dinghies). State law may require a number displayed on the hull even on the smallest boats.
Licenses (if applicable)	All (stored at home for dinghies)
Ship's logs	All (stored at home for dinghies)
Manuals for all equipment	All (stored at home for dinghies)
Identification papers for each person	All

DITCH BAG

This should be called an "abandon ship" bag. Everything needed to help you survive the rare need to abandon ship should be included in a waterproof, floating bag. Contents vary but should include water, food, medical supplies, and communication devices.

Boat Type
Cruising class

ROPES, FIBER TYPES, AND THEIR USES

All must be correctly sized, both length and diameter, for the task each is to perform. All ropes and sails will be synthetic.

Nylon

This fiber is useful where stretch is desirable. Mooring lines and anchor rodes benefit from stretchiness. This reduces the sudden shock when the line is pulled on hard and can help protect the boat. (All anchors should have chain attached to them. After a length of chain, many opt for nylon to make up the rest of the rode.) Spinnakers are usually made of nylon.

Polypropylene

This fiber has limited use shipboard, because it is not strong and lacks resistance to sunlight. Still, it can last for a few years especially in northern climes, and it is resistant to rot. Its great advantage is it floats. This makes it useful for towing a dinghy, because there is less risk of the line wrapping around the propeller. It is never used for anchor lines, because it tends to pull the anchor up.

Less stretchy ropes

We want ropes that do not stretch for handling sails. When the wind comes up, we do not want the line to stretch past the point we want the sail set. That will make the sail baggy just when we want it slimmed. Also, we want the sail's power transferred to the boat without the loss from stretchiness. So for sail handling, the less stretch the better.

POLYESTER. Usually encountered under the DuPont trade name "Dacron," it is overall a first choice for cruisers for its characteristics of reasonable price, good strength, low stretch, and good resistance to sunlight, rot, and abrasion. Some varieties can be very low in stretch, and others can contain a mix of fibers, although at a greater cost. Dacron is also commonly used in cruising sails. An upgrade for lesser stretch in sails is to use polyester as a film, called Mylar®. Exotic materials, or carbon fiber, are also used in low-stretch racing sails.

Very low-stretch ropes

For lower stretch and lighter weight, there are a number of more exotic and expensive materials. For halyards in particular, these can be chosen by the cruiser as well as the racer. Cruisers find it desirable to set and forget the halyards, whereas sheets are easier and quicker to adjust. Examples of exotic materials are *aramids* like Technora®, Kevlar®, and a type of improved polyethylene called Spectra®. Sometimes a mix of fibers is utilized in one rope to obtain the desired combination of low stretch, resistance to abrasion, good handling, and cost. Synthetic ropes can be stronger and less stretchy for their weight than steel.

Other fiber use

Some other fibers are used in other areas of the boat. Carbon can be used to stiffen a hull and strengthen it and also can be used in sails. Fiberglass obviously is used extensively. Kevlar is stronger than fiberglass. These are bound in various materials like polyester resin, which can absorb some water and result in blistering. Polyvinyl esters and epoxy can be used for greater strength and water resistance.

SMART PHONES AND GPS

iPhone and Android both have an overwhelming number of sailing applications downloadable, some for free, some at a cost. These include navigation charts and software, communications, rules, and safety.

I can envision the day in the near future in which all electronic functions shipboard are served by smart phones telling us wind speed and direction, boat speed and direction, engine coolant temperature, bilge water level, holding tank level, whether the boat is properly moored, whether anyone has boarded her or attempted to board her, and maybe even allowing the boat to send a message to the owner, such as, "I miss you," or perhaps, "I'm sorry, Dave, I'm afraid I can't do that." A smart phone GPS may be very useful as a backup. The charts and maps must be on the phone, because you may sail out of the cell phone's range.

Any electronic device designed for home, auto, or other land-based use is unlikely to survive a soaking. There are covers available to protect these. Many of the covers allow for the use of the touch-screen functions. You can also use a watertight sandwich bag, although a good case will be more durable and better protect the equipment.

The features of a highway GPS are not the same as the features needed in a marine GPS. A highway GPS may be designed to allow navigation only to an address or intersection and may not be sufficiently water-resistant. A highway GPS may not have a COB or MOB (crew overboard or man overboard) button, which gives a distance and direction readout to the location you were at when, as soon as possible after the event, you pressed a single button to indicate where the crew overboard was. If you are purchasing a GPS, see that, in addition to having a COB or MOB function, it allows a read-out of compass direction, and position in the traditional latitude and longitude format of hours, minutes, and seconds, critical for rescue services to locate you. See also that it will allow you to input the location of a mark, such as a navigation buoy.

CRUISING BOAT MAINTENANCE

REPAIR SAFETY

You will need to maintain your boat. In Day Four, we covered inspection of the rigging, the hull, the sails, flares, lights, fuel tank, engine oil, steering, propane heating and cooking systems. We learned to listen for changes in the engine sounds and how to do a radio check. This appendix adds repair safety considerations, hull repair, bottom paint, mast tuning, plumbing issues, battery maintenance, electrolysis, below decks mechanisms, and the creation of an owner's log.

1. Check to see the boat is safe to work on. Is it tied securely? If on land, is it secured so it cannot tip? If the boat is on jackstands, are the jackstands secured by chain to one another to keep them from tipping or sliding around? Can they slip? If on a cradle, is the cradle in good shape?

2. Trailers pose particular dangers. The bow's jack has limited strength; do not exceed it by having too many people or too much weight on the foredeck. Worse, a trailer alone has no protection against tipping to the rear. Move your 200 pounds to the stern to put on the 75-pound outboard, and you may have 2,750 foot pounds of force ready to tip the boat and trailer. Imagine the bow tipping to the point it contacts overhead wires, or till it spills you and the boat off

the trailer. Chock the wheels securely, and add at least one pair of well secured jackstands or other secure braces at the stern. Secure the trailer to the tow vehicle for added solidity. Set the parking brake, lock the tow vehicle, and take all the car keys with you.

TOOL SAFETY

There are some particularized tool safety issues in the marine environment.

1. Never use a corded (household or greater voltage) tool on a boat unless it is on dry land. Cordless tools operate on safer DC current and at lower voltages. Even in the relative safety of the cabin, electrocution is a real possibility in the damp environment. Turning off the tool will not prevent electrocution if you drop it in any water.
2. Be very cautious using sharp tools. It will take far longer to get to a hospital from your boat than from your home.
3. When working with sharp tools, have an assistant with you, even as an observer. If you fall, or injure yourself, how will you even get to shore?
4. Keep your cell phone, if in range, and your marine radio handy.
5. A magnet may help you recover parts that fall into the bilge and, if on a rope, can help recover tools or keys that have fallen overboard.

MAST CLIMBING

1. Never climb the mast if there is any possible way to avoid it. Look up the mast. See if there is a way to clear that tangle or make that repair from the deck. Maybe you can snag that errant halyard with your boat hook. Maybe there is a higher seawall in your harbor, so arranged and high enough to safely reach the repair.
2. Always think safety first if you must climb the mast.
3. Be sure that your weight at the top of the mast will not flip the boat over. If you with your tools and boson's chair weigh 200 pounds, that means 6,000 foot pounds are at the top of a 30-foot mast. Is your keel's ballast well over 6,000 foot pounds? It isn't in many boats. Assume it isn't in your boat.
4. You can reduce your chance of serious injury by using a proper boson's chair, mast steps, or a TopClimber.

5. Never climb the mast using just one halyard as a support for yourself. Add a second halyard as a safety line. Keep the safety line taught enough that if the first halyard lets go, you will not fall far. Add a third rope around the mast also secured to you. This will slow your fall a bit, and stop you at the next set of spreaders. It will also keep you from swaying out from the mast. I assume your idea of a fun sail doesn't involve imitating a pendulum for the rest of your (possibly short) life.

6. It is particularly hazardous to climb a mast to repair a broken stay or shroud. The mast must first be secured with a halyard subbing for the broken stay. By secured, that means winched tight and tied off. That leaves one less halyard to secure you. Do not climb without both a primary and a secondary safety halyard.

HULL REPAIR AND MAINTENANCE

1. Fiberglass repair techniques are covered by several manufacturers and authors. All will advise the use of respirators when sanding. Gloves are essential; allergies can develop from contact with epoxy.

2. Bottom paint is a biocide and therefore a biohazard. Wear a respirator, protect your skin, and vacuum up as you sand. Lay plastic underneath the boat to catch falling paint. Dispose of the residue in a responsible manner.

3. Rudder and Keel: Follow professional advice on inspecting and maintaining these.

TUNING THE RIG

Most boats have wires holding up the mast. The ones in front and back are called stays. The ones to the side are called shrouds.

Once the rig is verified secure and safe as described in Day Three, it can be *tuned*. This is the application of tension in the right amount. There is an art to the amount of tension to put on the rig, within certain parameters. The rig must be tight enough that the mast is never free to sway. Even if in the harbor the mast cannot sway, it can still be too loose to be safe. Picture putting 15 knots of wind on all your sails: that will push the mast to one side a bit. Even then, the leeward shrouds should have some tension on them. Otherwise, when the tension comes off, as in a tack, the mast will slap to one side, putting a shock load on the entire rig. On the other hand, if the rig is too tight, it puts excessive stress on the hull itself and can permanently bend the hull. If you do not feel comfortable just estimating the right amount of tension (you will have plenty of company in this), your sailmaker or another source can tell you how many pounds of tension to use (there are meters to help you) or simply tell you how many fractions of an inch each wire should deflect under a certain amount of pressure.

Tuning begins with the mast straight up from side to side and light and equal tension on the stays and shrouds. Then, tighten the wires going to the top of the mast, and then work on the ones going to the next highest point, and so on. Tighten each side equally by keeping track of the number of turns made on the turnbuckles. Go back and forth from side to side after just a few turns. Do not turn one side tight without turning the other side an equal amount, and tighten it bit by bit. As a rough rule, tighten the rig enough that when the boat is heeled 15 or even 20 degrees, there is still slight tension on the wires to leeward. If you find the need to take in some turns on the shrouds to leeward, take in the same number of turns on the shrouds on the other side.

Tighten the forestay and backstay to about the same tension as the shrouds. Often, you may want to tilt the mast backwards a bit at the top. That can increase windward helm, a condition that, within limits, is desirable.

Make sure all the running rigging (the ropes that hoist, lower, and control the sails) is in like-new condition. Replace any worn ropes. The old line can be used as a "messenger" for the new, which will allow the new rope to be pulled up the mast, around the mast pulleys at the top (*sheaves*), and back to the deck, a much easier proposition than trying to feed it through by itself, which can only be done at the top of the mast using gravity—the same thing that can pull you down from there and kill you.

Check the sails. That thread that has come loose can be fixed for a few dollars now. Better yet, have your local sailmaker check each sail.

MARINE HEAD ISSUES

The most frequent issues are odors and poor flushing. There is a "joker" or "duckbill" valve at the sewage output at the base of the head. It is the most frequent source of poor flushing by a marine head. Have a spare. Some suggest flushing a tablespoon of cooking oil a few times each year, which will lubricate that valve, extending its life. This valve is easy enough to reach but revolting to replace. Have the holding tank pumped out before working on the head.

Add a filter to the holding tank vent line to eliminate odors. Use sanitation-grade hoses. If you wipe the hose with a cloth, and it picks up an odor, the hose is done for, and the odor cannot be eliminated without replacing that hose. The use of seawater for flushing can itself be a source of odor. Consider connecting a freshwater input line. Use a good grade tank chemical. Avoid the use of a tank chemical with formaldehyde. Formaldehyde smells and requires a strong "perfume" to cover its odor. It is also a carcinogen.

OTHER PLUMBING ISSUES

It is not recommended to have a shore-water hose connected to the boat. A plumbing leak can sink the boat. Rely instead on your boat's internal tank. Of course, the tank should be clean. It will have a vent. A screen, or better yet a filter, should be at the vent to prevent insects and dirt from entering. Shore water should be filtered before it is allowed into the tank. The water may sit in the tank for weeks or longer; consider using a potable water chemical.

BATTERIES

Do you see corrosion on the battery? If so, remove the cables, clean, and reattach. Cover the battery terminals with grease. Check the voltage. A fully charged standard lead-acid 12-volt battery should read about 12.6 to 12.7 volts after brief use. The engine alternator should put out at least 14.1 volts at the battery during the charging phase. The exact minimum is disputed. If the voltage from the charger drops below that at the battery but is sufficient at the engine, the wiring is inadequate. The simple way to fix that is to put in parallel wires of the correct gauge. The maximum charging voltage at the battery is also a matter of dispute, but very few authorities would suggest that a maximum charging voltage of 14.3 volts would reduce battery life.

The different battery manufacturers cite different charging regimens. For longest battery life, make sure your alternator and charger follow that exact regimen; many smart types are user-adjustable. One manufacturer states a full charge is when the charger is at 14.4 volts, and the battery is accepting only one to two percent of its capacity (e.g., a 100-amp hour battery is accepting only one or two amperes). The fully charged battery should then be placed on a "float charge" at 13.7 volts. This regimen requires too much engine use; you will want solar cells, a wind generator, and/or a shore-power charger. Using the engine solely to charge, most sailors bring the batteries up to only an 80 percent charge. It takes a long time for the last 20 percent of battery charge to take place.

ELECTRICAL LEAKAGE AND ELECTROLYSIS

The shore-power system must be grounded and isolated properly. An expert should check this out. Power leaks can cause metals to degrade, destroy your boat, and, worse, kill swimmers.

Zincs, as they are generically called, protect other metal parts and must be replaced when one half used up. Zincs for freshwater use are actually magnesium, and for brackish water may be aluminum. The metals for zincs are never mixed. It is particularly essential to protect the lower unit of a sail drive. These aluminum units are particularly vulnerable to electrolysis. Severe electrolysis is often caused by the lack of a proper galvanic isolator on the electrical system. It can be from a nearby boat.

MAINTENANCE OF BELOW DECK MECHANISMS

In Day Four, the eighteenth step, we learned a bit about seacocks. A more thorough servicing of these is in order. If the boat is on land, service the seacocks as recommended in their manual. If in the water, service them to the extent possible. If water starts coming in, the first thing you will do is close all valves (except engine water valves if an inboard engine is running). Check each and every clamp annually and tighten if necessary. When replacing these because of corrosion, etc., make sure that both the clamp and its screw are stainless steel. A good grade of stainless is not attracted to a magnet, making it easy to verify. Label each through-hull fitting with paint, indicating what each is for. It is good practice to shut all valves when leaving the boat for a period of time. If you have gate valves, replace those with proper seacocks during your next haul-out. A gate valve is the type that is used to turn on and off ordinary garden hoses; it requires several turns to shut off. You cannot tell just by looking that it is shut. When replacing through-hulls, some prefer to use a marine plywood base to spread the load of the tightened bolts around a greater area of fiberglass. Check that wood, and all other structural plywood, for rot. Push a screwdriver into any questionable parts. Weak wood will reveal itself then.

Check the bilge pump(s). Pour a little water in the hull. See to it that the pump starts manually and actually pumps out water. Make sure the pump doesn't get very hot to the touch. The pump may also operate automatically. Test it either by flipping an apparent float valve up or pouring enough water in the bottom to activate it. Put a plug in any sink. A sink can ship water when the boat is heeling.

BOAT MAINTENANCE AND NAVIGATION LOG

This can be as simple or as complex as you wish. In its simplest form, it can be a standard three-ring binder, containing all of the instruction and maintenance manuals for your boat, together with a list of things to do before fall storage and at spring recommissioning; magazine articles; sailing destinations and lessons learned ("when we reefed the main at 17 knots and three-foot waves, our speed dropped only 0.1 knot and the ride was much more comfortable"); notes about any harbor approaches (viz., "be sure to leave the Michigan City breakwall to starboard when entering"); repairs completed; projects for the next lay-up; dates of repairs, fueling, and battery charging. Your log and ink should be waterproof.

APPENDIX F

THE PHYSICS OF HOW YOUR SAILS MOVE THE BOAT

This is not the traditional explanation of how sails work. It is the accurate and useful one. Once you understand how sails operate, you will more easily spot and correct deficiencies, just like an automobile mechanic can fix a car and make it run better, faster, smoother.

You will recall the general principle of sail trim: let it out until it luffs, and pull it back in until the sail just fills. If you ask sailors how the sails work, or read another how-to-sail book, 90 percent of them will reference Bernoulli's Principle. Teaching how Bernoulli's Principle will help you adjust sails is never made clear. I'm with the 10 percent. I think the sails' operation is best explained differently. I expect to be with the 90 percent, maybe the 100 percent, in a few years.

It is easy to see how a pedal can turn a sprocket, which moves a chain, which turns another sprocket, which turns a wheel, moving a bike. It is equally easy to see how a turning engine can turn a car's wheels. Our brains have been trained over time to understand this intuitively. Air is invisible, so our brains have received less training to understand how things move in air. You are about to learn to visualize how the wind going across the sail moves the boat. Operating the sails will become intuitive. Then sail control becomes simple. Remove the mystery, replace it with understanding, and you will be able to act and react correctly, swiftly, and confidently.

Let's start with a couple of experiments.

EXPERIMENT NO. 1. You are familiar with what happens if you stick your hand out a window of a moving car. The wind will push your hand back. But, if you tilt your hand palm up, the air will push your hand up. It is an equal but opposite reaction, as Isaac Newton taught us. Your hand is forcing the air to change direction, only slightly downward. The air then forces your hand up (Figure 8.2). Try it also in the opposite direction. You will also notice that, regardless of the wind direction and speed felt in a stationary car, the wind is almost always directly in front of the swiftly moving car. The former is the actual wind. The latter is the apparent wind, shifted forward by any moving object.

EXPERIMENT NO. 2. Now try an experiment with a metal spoon and a faucet. With the water running, move the spoon to the water flow, with the "fat" (convex) side closer to the water. Hold the spoon loosely to allow it to sway. Watch what happens as you slowly move the spoon into the water.

Figure 8.2. (Drawing by Clare Rosean)

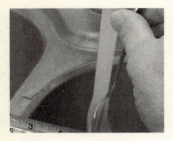

Figure 8.3.
Spoon in water
stream.

Did you see the water touch the spoon? Did you see the water immediately "decide" to follow the curve of the spoon? And, you saw the spoon move into the flow of water on its own. The water had to follow the curve of the spoon. That caused the water to move a bit away from its original direction. At the tip of the spoon, the water is moved away from the main stream. The equal but opposite reaction made the spoon move into the water with a force strong enough to partly overcome the water's attempt to push it out of the stream (see Figure 8.3).

The water stream was near the 5 ½"-mark, when the spoon and stream are not affecting one another. As soon as the spoon made contact with the stream, the water curved along its surface, bending the stream. The equal but opposite reaction moved the spoon about three-quarters of an inch.

Can you see where we are going with this?

Every object on earth can move only in accordance with Newton's Laws of Motion. We only need to know a little about just one of the three laws. For us, it is enough to know that for every action on an object, there is an equal but opposite reaction. We are all familiar with this. It is more obvious in some situations than others. Blow up a balloon and release it without tying it shut. You know what happens. In a propeller airplane, you intuitively know the wind coming off the propeller pushes the aircraft forward. Powerboats, with their propellers, push water backwards, which pushes the boat forward. While these are obvious examples, some are more subtle. Nothing can be moved on earth unless something acts on it, which causes an equal but opposite reaction. Airplanes and sailboats are not immune to this physical law: they are bound to it and controlled by it. It is easy to see how a propeller can move a boat. It is not as obvious how a stationary piece of cloth can move enough air to move the boat.

Every sail works by bending the wind. When the wind is bent by the sail from its original direction to a direction a bit more toward the rear of the boat, it pushes the boat forward just as a propeller blowing in that direction would. That is Newton's Third Law of Motion in actual use on a sailboat. For every action, there is an equal but opposite reaction.

EXPERIMENT NO. 3. Securely attach a stout string to a ball. Swing it around. Vary the speed. What you should see is the ball travelling in a curve, forming a circle. What you will feel is the string pulling on you. It is pulling on you with a force related to the weight of the ball and the speed with which it is turning. Think about that. When the air curves around the sail, it pulls on the sail with the force related to the speed and amount of air moved. It is felt like suction on the sails. The more air we turn, and the faster it goes, the greater the force on the sail. With the ball on a string, swinging in all directions, the force pulls in all directions. But the sails apply force only in certain directions. And as the forward direction force of the sails increases, the force causing the boat to tip also increases. We need a happy medium.

With that in mind, let's take a closer look at some of the ways to push an engineless boat forward:

1. Step off it. That pushes it away. Try this with a small dinghy, making sure you don't land in the water, and you will clearly see an equal but opposite reaction.
2. Attach a fan to it, aiming rearward. That will push air backwards, and thus the boat will go forward.
3. Attach a sail to it, and use it to bend the wind to push backwards. (see Figure 8.4).

Notice how the wind in Figure 3.4 (Day Three) is facing the sail. Notice the wind is directly striking the front of the sail. The wind needs to strike the inside of the sail with enough force to "inflate" it, filling the sail with wind (compare Figure 3.5). The wind on the outside of the sail is particularly important. The wind on the outside of the sail is most effective

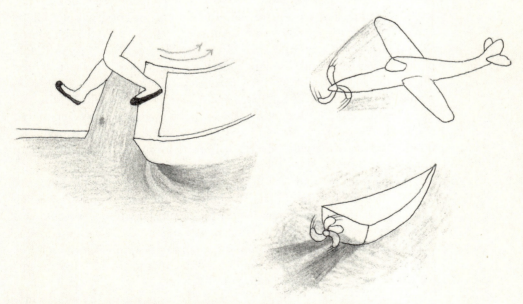

Figure 8.4. A. Person stepping off dinghy, pushing it back. B. Propeller pushing air back, driving the aircraft forward. C. Fan attached to a boat, pushing air back, driving the boat forward. The sails do the same thing. They push air back, driving the boat forward. (Drawing by Clare Rosean)

if it strikes the outside front of the sail from the smallest angle possible. So the sail works best if the wind comes at it at a point just allowing the sail to inflate or fill.

Sail adjustment with these concepts is easy. This is why, as mentioned in Day One, regardless of the direction of the wind relative to the boat, the apparent wind direction relative to the sail is kept constant! Your objective: let the sail just fill with wind by aiming the very front edge of the sail's curve into the wind, with just enough wind underneath it to fill it. Limitations of the boat make for certain compromises. For example, you don't want the sail to rub on the wires holding the mast, so the sail can only go so far out from the centerline of the boat.

But, how can this sail which is just sitting there on the boat propel a boat weighing tons forward? The answer is the sail moves a lot of air. The typical illustrations in a how to sail book show only a small amount of air, right near the sail, being affected by the sail. But, if you talk to those who have successfully raced sailboats, they can tell you how far away their boat is affected by the wind off another boat's sail. A boat's sail noticeably affects the wind hundreds of feet away. Many estimate the effect is significant at a distance 7 times the height of the sail. For example, a popular 30 foot long sailboat that has a 44 foot mast (and sail), the wind is affected about 300 feet away. Its sail area is 446 square feet. The astonishing total: about 130,000 cubic feet of air is affected by your small boat's sail. So, even though a cubic foot of air weighs very little, that 130,000 cubic feet of air weighs 10,000 pounds! Even if you take a more conservative figure for the distance from the sail the air is affected by it, say three times the mast height, over 4,000 pounds of air is moved. And that is just the air on the "outside" of the sail. There is also air going along the inside of the sail which is also being moved rearward. We will focus for simplicity on the outside, letting the inside airflow just take care of itself. How is a sail able to move all that air which is not touching it? You have heard that nature "abhors a vacuum."

Again, refer to Figure 3.4 in Day Three. At top left is a typical illustration of wind being bent by a sail: it shows a curved line, commonly called an *airstream*. The air must remain near the sail. Otherwise there would be a vacuum between it and the sail, which nature abhors . . . the vacuum, that is, not the sail. We can think of air near the sail as a stream, even though it is formed of tiny little molecules. Engineers often use the concept of airstreams for visualization purposes; we can, too.

At top right the next level of air, or airstream, across the sail is illustrated. The adjacent curved airstream must stay as close as it can to the first airstream. Otherwise, there would be a vacuum between the first airstream and the second.

On the main illustration, we see that each adjacent curved line, a representation of an airstream, must stay next to its neighbor in turn, to avoid a vacuum. The curving effect diminishes very gradually. If that little bit of wind adjacent to the sail in the top left illustration was all the air the sail affected, the "new world" wouldn't have been "discovered" in the age of sail. There couldn't even be an age of sail. No sailboat could really move. It would violate Newton's laws. Good luck trying to get anything to move without complying with that guy's laws.

But if the air particles next to that little bit of wind didn't follow the same path as their neighbors', a vacuum would exist; yes, a partial vacuum, but a vacuum nonetheless. So the air particles just have to follow their neighbors pretty much in lockstep, like well-trained marchers. And so on and so on and so on for "layer" after "layer" and stream after stream as shown in the illustration. Physicists, please don't write to me about Einstein's modification of Newton's laws (which we call Relativity), turbulence, or Heisenberg's Uncertainty Principle. If you can get your sailboat to travel at such high speeds that Relativity is relevant, you do not need this book. Turbulence is covered later in these pages; I am certain Heisenberg's Principle is not.

Now, picture the smooth curve of your sail, and picture all that air flowing past, changing direction more toward the aft as it goes across the sail, and you can see how we will make our sailboat move. It just requires us to get the wind flowing more in a direction to the rear of the boat than it was before. Once we do that, smoothly, nature takes over and sends the air in lockstep. We didn't need to move it all the way aft, just a bit, like the spoon in our experiment was enough. Meanwhile the keel and the rudder, combine to force the boat to go in the chosen direction. Once you understand this, you begin to know how to adjust the sails, intuitively, in most conditions.

As long as the wind can follow the shape of the sail, the wind will smoothly flow across it. To the extent the wind curves smoothly aft, those 4,000 pounds of air mass will cause that now familiar equal but opposite reaction, moving the boat forward. Unfortunately, your sailboat cannot successfully bend the wind even 90 degrees from its original direction. It can only successfully bend the wind aft gently, and smoothly, along a slight curve. If you try to bend the wind too much, the sail will stall, much like an airplane wing can. You won't crash, but the boat will slow down—a lot. This is an example of turbulence. The air, instead of generally smoothly turning aft, forms eddies and whirlpools that do not help the sailboat move because they are not moving in the proper direction, reducing the forward force the sail creates. (It doesn't matter whether you perceive this force as suction on the sail or the force of the air being deflected to the back of the boat. The force of the suction is equal to the force of

Figure 8.5. (Photo courtesy of Paul Bowen)

Figure 8.5. (Photo courtesy of Paul Bowen)

the air being deflected rearward. It is another application of a Newtonian equal but opposite reaction.)

This is the same force that holds helicopters and airplanes up. In the case of helicopters, everyone fully understands that the air is being forced in

the same thing.

When the sail is pulled in too tight, it will look good but not work its

GLOSSARY

actual wind. The wind felt by motionless instruments, people, or boats. See also *apparent wind*.

aft. A direction, to the rear of the boat, or behind the rear of the boat.

apparent wind. A wind you feel, or experience. It is different from the *actual wind* because the boat's forward motion adds to or subtracts from the *actual wind* and changes its direction.

astern. Also a direction, behind the rear of the boat.

backstay. The metal wire running from the top—or near the top—of the *mast* to the *stern*. It is an essential structural support for the *mast*.

backstay adjuster. A device that can increase tension on the *backstay*. This can actually bend the mast *aft*, which has the effect of flattening the main, especially at its *luff*, and can exert tension on the *forestay*, if the *forestay* is connected at about the same height on the *mast* as the *backstay*.

barberhauler. A line connected to a sheet to pull the sheet and sail, usually inward.

beam. The width of the boat; the widest part of the boat.

bearing. A direction, usually the direction from the boat; sometimes the direction from an object.

bear off . Adjust heading by turning away from the direction of the wind. Also called *fall off*.

bend on. The process of attaching the sails to the rigging.

blanketing. Blocking the wind from a sail.

boardboat. A *dinghy* with only a shallow footwell rather than a full cockpit.

boom. A horizontal spar that helps controls the shape of the mainsail.

bow. The pointed front part of the boat.

Bowline Hitch (*bo-lin*). The most important single knot to learn because it can be used for many purposes.

bridle. A line connecting the two bows of a *catamaran* to the anchor's rode.

catamaran. A multi-hulled watercraft featuring two parallel hulls of equal size.

centerboard. A lightweight *keel*, which can usually be lifted to reduce draft. It resists the sideways force of the sails. It is not adequate to resist the heeling force from the sails.

centerline. An imaginary line from the *bow* through the *mast* to the center of the rear of the boat.

chainplate. Metal custom fabrications connecting the *turnbuckles* and rigging to the *hull* of the boat.

chart. A nautical map.

Cleat Hitch. A knot to tie a line to a cleat.

clew. The rear bottom corner of a sail to which *sheets* are attached.

close hauled. Sailing in a direction as close to *upwind* as is possible to sail effectively.

Clove Hitch. A two-loop simple knot.

COLREGS. International Regulations for Preventing Collisions at Sea.

companionway. The entrance to the cabin from the cockpit.

contour lines. Most *charts* have individual depth readings at indicated points. Others have a line of equal depth marked on the chart together with the individual depth readings. Important contour lines can be drawn by you following the charted depths.

cringle. A reinforced (often metal) hole in a sail. This is used to secure the sail to the *mast*, *boom*, or *ropes*. *Cringles* are usually found at the *clew*, the *tack*, the *head*, and *reef* points. Not all *cringles* are in use at all times.

cunningham. A line at the bottom front of a *mainsail*, usually connected to the *mast*, used to pull down and flatten the front of the sail.

daggerboard. A form of *keel* that generally is straight and narrow like a dagger. Usually it can be raised and lowered. Often, it has little or no ballast.

daymark. A form of unlit navigation aid.

dinghy. As used in this text, it is a 6- to 20-foot long sailboat with a *centerboard* or *daggerboard* and no heavy *keel*. It is not self-righting in the event of a capsize.

downwind. A heading wherein the wind is coming more from *astern* than from the front or side.

dousing. Lowering the sail. Opposite of *hoisting*.

draft. The depth of the lowest part of the *keel*.

electrolysis. Corrosion below the waterline whenever dissimilar metals are in proximity.

fall off. See *bear off*.

fetch. An *upwind* heading that will just allow a sailboat to reach its destination without *tacking*.

fitting. Used herein to refer to any solid part used to connect one part, or *rope*, to the deck, a sail, or another part.

foil. A more general term than airfoil. This refers to the shape and effect of the sails, *keel*, and *centerboard*. Their shape contributes to the flow of water or air around them, making them more effective at their jobs than a flat surface.

foot. Bottom part of the sail. Also sometimes used to mean *bear off* (*foot* off).

foredeck. The general area of the front of the boat. The *foredeck* crew position requires the most strength and agility of all, with the possible exception of those handling specialized winches on elite racing boats.

foresail. Any and all sails attached in front of the *mast*: *jib*, *genoa*, or *spinnaker*.

forestay. The metal wire running from the top of the *mast* (or near the top of the *mast*) to the *bow*. It is an essential structural support for the *mast* on most sailboats.

freeboard. The height of the boat's sides above the waterline. Those boards are "free," not being directly needed for flotation and available to do work keeping the boat dry.

gaff rig. A sailboat whose *mainsail* has a solid beam at the top. Thus, the sail forms more of a rectangular shape than a triangular shape. It allows for more *mainsail* area down low for less *heeling*, but it is not considered as efficient as a *sloop* rig for *upwind* sailing.

give-way. The boat which must maneuver to keep clear of the *stand-on* vessel to avoid collision.

genoa. A *foresail* that overlaps the mainmast.

ground tackle. Mooring equipment such as anchors, *rode,* and chains.

guy. A *sheet*, except the *guy* is the rope that looks just like a *sheet* but is connected to the *spinnaker* and the *pole*, then led to the boat and winch.

halyard. The line that hauls a sail up.

handicap. A type of racing that attempts to make racing unequal boats more fair by penalizing faster boats a certain amount of time per mile of the race.

hank. A fitting in the shape of a piston with a hook on the end used to bend on a jib to a wire forestay.

hard on the wind. See *pointing*.

head. A bathroom on a boat. Also, the top of a sail.

head up. Turn the boat more in the direction toward the wind.

head down. Turn the boat further away from the direction the wind is coming from.

headboard. A strong fitting at the *head* of a sail to spread the load from the *halyard* to a larger area of the sail. Usually found on *mainsails*.

header. A wind shift that causes the boat to sail further away from the destination unless the boat is tacked.

heel. The tilt or lean to the side of a sailboat caused by the wind on the sails.

hitch. A knot intended to tie a line to an object. Examples: *Bowline Hitch, Clove Hitch*.

holding ground. The nature of a seabed for anchoring.

hoist. Raise the sail or anchor. Opposite of *douse,* when referring to a sail.

hull. The main body of the boat. As used in this text, it can apply also to fittings solidly attached to the hull.

impeller. A rubber water pump that pumps coolant through the engine.

jackline. This line is for the sailors to clip their harnesses to, securing them to the boat as they may move about.

jib. A *foresail* that does not overlap the mainmast.

jibe. A turn with the wind astern, during which the sails are switched from one side to the other. It is different from a tack, because in a tack the wind is in front of the boat.

kedging. Taking an anchor in a dinghy in the direction of your best exit from an obstruction, as far as possible, and setting it then winching it in to move the boat off the obstruction.

keel. A vertical, underwater *foil* that resists the force of the sails in two ways: side force and *heeling* force. Its weight helps keep the boat from *heeling*, and its surface area and *foil* shape help keep the boat on track *upwind*, resisting the side force. Often refers to all manner of underwater *foils*:

traditional ballasted *keels, centerboards,* and *daggerboards.*

keelboat. A sailboat with a heavy *keel* that makes the boat at least somewhat self-righting in the event of a capsize.

lazarette. A storage area *aft.* A cockpit locker.

leeway. Boat drift caused by wind and waves.

leeward. More downwind than *upwind* or to *windward.* Opposite of *windward.*

leech. The rear edge of the sail. It also can refer to much of the rear portion of a sail.

life vest. The common term for a personal flotation device (*PFD*).

lift. A wind change that turns your boat to a heading taking you closer to your destination.

luff. (n) The front or windward edge of the sail. For example, a symmetrical *spinnaker* can be thought of as having two *luffs,* but only one at a time is called "the *luff*." (v) turn the boat toward the wind.

luffing. The sail flapping in the wind.

mainsail. The sail behind the main mast.

mainsheet. The line that moves the mainsail in or out.

Marconi rig. See *sloop.*

mark. A certain location denoted by a point on a *chart,* or a navigation buoy.

mast. The tall, vertical, solid stick that holds up the sails.

navigation kit. The gear used to find your course and location.

no-go zone. The zone directly upwind and extending about 45 degrees on either side of your boat.

one-design. 1. A type of racing in which each boat is considered to be as fast as every other because they are of similar or identical designs. 2. The boats themselves so raced.

open shore. The shoreline along a body of water that is not affected by a bay or other restriction of current, tides, or waves.

osmotic blisters. Blisters in the outer surface of a fiberglass hull caused by water seeping into the fiberglass below the waterline.

outhaul. A line at the bottom rear of the *mainsail,* connected to the *boom,* used to pull the main out, flattening its bottom.

pelorus. A device through which you can sight angles.

PFD. Personal flotation device, acronym for a *life vest* or life jacket.

pinching. Sailing a boat a little more upwind than is optimal.

pointing. The ability of a boat to aim close to the wind direction. The act of heading *upwind* to the maximum *upwind* speed.

pole. Usually a *spar* used to support and control the *spinnaker.*

port. The left side of the boat when looking forward.

port tack. Navigating your boat when the wind is coming over the boat's *port* side and the boom is out to *starboard.*

reef. Reduce sail area, by lowering the sail. Usually this is done on the *mainsail.* Infrequently, *jibs* have *reef* points. *Mainsails* may have multiple *reef* points.

reeve. Run a line through the proper pulleys, fairleads, stoppers, etc.

rigging. Rigging includes all of the boat parts that handle the sails.

rode. The anchor chain and/or line.

rope. Landlubber's term for lines, *halyards,* etc.

rpms. Revolutions per minute. The basic measure of engine speed.

rudder. Underwater device, near the *stern* turned by a tiller or wheel to steer the boat.

sacrificial zincs. Sacrificial metal used to protect your critical metals like bolts, shafts, and engine lower units from corrosion.

sailplan. The basic design of the sails, their height, and width as drawn on a flat sheet of paper.

scull. Rapidly swinging the rudder back and forth to move the boat forward.

sea anchor. A parachute dragging in the water, set from the *bow*. It holds the *bow* into the wind and into any breaking waves.

sheet. A line that hauls sails in and out.

sheet in. Pull on the line that hauls the sail in and out.

sheet out. Let out some of the line that hauls the sail in and out.

shroud. A wire that connects the side of the *mast* to the side of the boat. There may be several on each side: one at the *mast head*, and one at the base of each *spreader*. The *spreader* may have fore and *aft* lower *shrouds*.

sloop. A type of sailboat, with one sail in front of the *mast* and one behind, forming a triangle. Also known as a *Marconi rig*.

slot. The gap between the *foresail* and *mainsail*.

snubber. A stretchy, strong, often rubberized item that connects the boat to a mooring line or *rode*. This reduces stress on other *fittings*.

SOLAS-Safety of Life at Sea. The acronym is actually that of a convention of standards for safety equipment.

sounding. A term for the depth indication on a *chart*.

spar. The *boom* and the *mast*, and sometimes other long, rounded supports for *rigging*, such as a gaff or a yard.

spinnaker. A big, usually colorful *foresail*.

spreader. Horizontal *fittings* sticking out from the *mast* to either side. There can be several, sometimes none.

spring lines. Long lines used in tying to a dock.

splice. A permanent weaving of a line to another (or to itself to secure a *fitting*).

stand-on. The vessel that may maintain course and speed but still must avoid collision with the give-way vessel.

starboard. The right side of the boat when looking forward.

starboard tack. Navigating your boat when the wind is coming over the boat's *starboard* side and the boom is out to port.

stay. A line, usually of wire that supports the mast. The line that leads from the top of the mast to the center of the stern is called the *backstay*. The line that leads from the mast to the bow is called the *forestay*.

step. A strong *fitting* on which the base, or bottom, of the *mast* rests.

stern. The rear of the boat.

Stopper Knot. A figure-eight knot to keep a rope from going through a *fitting*.

swing keel. A type of *keel* in a trailerable sailboat. It provides some ballast and will require a winch to raise it.

tabernacle. A strong *fitting* to which the base or bottom of the *mast* is attached, similar to a *mast step*. The difference is that a *tabernacle* is designed to allow a *mast* to swing up, facilitating *mast*-raising on a trailerable boat.

tachometer. A gauge to indicate *rpms* on an engine.

tack. 1. The front, bottom corner of a sail; lines may be attached, but usually it is connected to a *fitting* on the boat. 2. The direction a boat is moving in. 3. A change in direction so that the wind goes from one side of the boat to the other.

tape. A reinforcing long, narrow length of sailcloth at the edges of a sail.

telltales. Narrow strips of cloth or yarn attached on one end only to a sail, that is used to indicate airflow.

thimble. An eye-shaped metal piece reinforcing an *eye splice*, connecting a *rode* to the anchor chain through a shackle. This reduces the chafing of the *rope* at the eye *splice*.

tiller. A stick attached to the top of a *rudder*, used to turn the *rudder*.

topping lift. A line that holds the boom off the deck when the sail is lowered.

tracking. The ability of a boat to maintain a course. All boats, and especially sailboats, are pushed a bit by the wind and waves in a direction other than desired. *Tracking* is the relative ability of a boat to continue on a desired course despite the wind and waves attempting to push it off course.

transom. The rear end of the *hull* of the boat.

trapeze. A system of wires going to the top of the *mast* to allow the sailors to suspend themselves over the water, so that they can balance the boat with their full weight.

traveler. A strong *fitting* going across the boat under the *boom*, equipped with a moveable fitting called a *traveler car*. This connects with the *mainsheet*.

trim. Adjust the sail to suit the conditions, first by adjusting the *sheet*. It can (less frequently) refer to the use of other controls, such as the *halyard*, *backstay adjuster*, etc.

trip line. A line attached to the anchor opposite the rode so if necessary the anchor can be hauled out the opposite way it came in.

true wind. The direction and speed of airflow at a nonmoving object. *Actual wind*.

tuning. The application of tension to the rig after the rig had been verified secure and safe.

turnbuckle. Tensioning device connecting each *stay* and *shroud* to the deck and *chainplates*.

upwind. A heading wherein the wind appears to be coming from ahead, or at least more forward than to the side or behind.

vang. A *fitting* or line that keeps the *boom* from rising. It performs the downward function of the *mainsheet*, taking over that function when the mainsheet is eased past the point at which it pulls strongly downward.

washboard. Akin to a Dutch door, these are usually in two parts, a lower and upper, that together form a door at the *companionway*. Usually they slide in, unlike Dutch doors, which swing open, and are removable.

waypoints. Turning points on your voyage.

weather window. A period of good weather to depart on a voyage.

windlass. A specialized winch for the anchor, often electrically powered.

windward. More toward the wind than downwind. Opposite of *leeward*. Similar to *upwind*.

RESOURCES

BOOKS

General Sailing

Chapman's Piloting. This is perhaps the ultimate reference for boating rules and safety.

A Boater's Guide to the Federal Requirements for Recreational Boats. http://www.uscgboating.org/assets/1/workflow_staging/Publications/420.PDF. Free.

U.S. Coast Guard Publication No. CG-172 for detailed navigation requirements. See also the latest edition of the *Rules of the Road*, available online.

Sailboats

Robert Perry. Author of at least six books entitled *Sailing Designs*, each containing reviews of about 250 boats. He will describe good and bad aspects of designs and recognizes innovation that he believes will work.

John Kretschmer. Author of several books, including *Used Boat Notebook*. He is biased toward good cruising designs and believes good design trumps good construction. He appreciates tracking ability over pointing ability, two related concepts. He points out that a very narrow, deep keel requires more speed to track well than a more conventional keel and picks some very interesting boats with a discussion of their strengths and weaknesses. Attend a lecture of his if you can; you will not regret it. Not a designer, he is a committed sailor who knows what he wants.

Knots

Clifford Ashley, *The Ashley Book of Knots*. Some consider this to be the ultimate guide to knots.

Airfoils

Abbot and Doenhoff, *Theory of Wing Sections*. This is a highly detailed, rather dense source. The 1959 edition is still available. If you are truing the keel, or rebuilding the rudder, it may help to understand those airfoils. The sails are also airfoils.

OTHER PRINT RESOURCES

Blue Water Sailor. A magazine dedicated to the cruiser. It has useful articles on destinations, maintenance, etc.

Cruising World. The name is self-explanatory.

Practical Sailor. An accurate source of unbiased information on boats and equipment. Like *Consumer Reports*, but strictly for boats. They can be fun; they like to try to break things. Usually not available in stores, but well worth the subscription. Or, order the most recent articles on the gear you are interested in.

Sail. One of the oldest continuously published sailing magazines.

Sailing. Very pretty pictures, and it hosts Robert Perry.

Sailing World. For the racer.

INTERNET

General Information

http://www.boat links.com/linklists/boatlink 25.html. The self-described mother of all maritime Internet links.

http://www.bateau.com/ Do you want to build your own boat? Some of these plans are free of charge.

www.nauticalcharts.noaa.gov and www.nauticalcharts.noaa.gov/mcd/OnLineViewer.html. The official U. S. marine charts covering all navigable waters.

Tidal Information

http://tidesite.appspot.com/ Pick your harbor; it will give details.

http://tidesandcurrents.noaa.gov. NOAA's official home page for tidal information.

Knots

There are nice sources on the Internet for videos showing how to tie knots. One such is http://www.animatedknots.com/bowlineboating/index.php. Another is Animated Knots by Greg http://www.animatedknots.com. The latter has an i-Phone app.

A general information website calling itself "The Interactive Cruising Guidebook" is available at www.activecaptain.com.

INDEX